BROOD BITCH

Brood Bitch

A Mother's Reflection

CELIA TOWNSEND WELLS

Purdue University Press
West Lafayette, Indiana

Printed in the United States of America

Library of Congress Cataloging-in-Publication Data

Wells, Celia Townsend, 1932–
    Brood bitch : a mother's reflection / Celia Townsend Wells.
        p.   cm.
    ISBN 1-55753-236-2 (cloth : alk. paper)
    1. Wells, Celia Townsend, 1932– 2. Dog breeders—Biography.
3. Pembroke Welsh corgi. 4. Human-animal relationships. 5. Mothers
and daughters. I. Title.
    SF422.82.W44 A3 2002
    636.7'082'092—dc21

                                        2002006871

For My Mother,
My Daughter,
and My Brood Bitch

Brood Bitch

··*1*··

*D*riving up the West Side Highway at five A.M. to Mt. Sinai Hospital I felt confident: my water had broken during the night and I was about to go into labor with my only child. I wasn't nervous or afraid; I was even calm. That was thirty-five years ago.

Driving up the Merritt Parkway at eight A.M. I also felt confident: my corgi bitch's water had broken an hour before, and my vet had arranged for me to whelp her at the hospital. I wasn't calm, but I wasn't worried. That was two years ago.

I have a married daughter, a maiden bitch, and a three-decade career as a university professor. Of these—there isn't a lot else in my life, a divorce having eventually proved that I prefer to live alone—my deepest commitment is to the corgi, whom I call Psallenda.

The name refers to a section in the vesper service of the Ambrosian chant, which is more elaborate than Gregorian. I was looking for one related to music and preferred the elaboration, the solemnity of vespers. While I am not religious, I like its similarity to the word "psalm," though I can't prove they have a common root, as "psallenda" is not recorded in either edition of the Oxford English Dictionary. That uniqueness ended my four-month quest to find just the right name for my special puppy.

We settled on Jennifer's name fairly early in my pregnancy; it was uncommon then, not showing up four times in a seminar of fifteen undergraduate women. It also had a possible literary origin in "Guinevere," which suited my specialization in medieval literature. We were hoping for a girl, but we had decided on Jason—equally classical—for a boy, just in case.

Before Poco's litter was born I had chosen several conductor's names for males: Esa-Pekka, Neemi, Sejei. That was what I wanted, a handsome stud dog like Poco's grandsire, Pesto. His registered name was "Pastime," and his daughter Tempo's was "Keep Time," starting the shift to musical terms over the generations. But there was only one male in Poco's litter and he wasn't my type—too plain, like Gregorian chant.

Although I didn't realize it before the birth of these puppies, I needed a bitch. I have always considered corgi males more devoted and less independent than females, but Psallenda is different. And though I preferred stud work to breeding litters—easier to get an excited call about nine weeks after a mating than agonize about the whelping and commit twelve weeks to raising the puppies—I changed my preference with this litter. The shift was unconscious at the time, rising from my feelings of thirty-five years as a mother.

Jennifer's birth was not easy; she was a breech, and after seventeen hours of labor, they put me under anesthetic and pulled her out. This is harder with puppies: there are more of them, and anesthesia is reserved for Caesarean sections, where it must be used cautiously. Purebred dogs do not have uncomplicated deliveries any more than human beings. But once their puppies are born, they are usually good mothers.

I wasn't. My calm on the West Side Highway was that before the proverbial storm. Although I had expressed some anxiety about becoming a "mother-woman," my husband was sure that would change after the baby came. But she cried a lot at times when we expected her to sleep, after she had been fed and freshly diapered, after a bath and cuddling, after we both kissed her good-night before going to bed. She didn't stop when I picked her up, she didn't want milk, she didn't need fresh diapers, she didn't like being rocked. Occasionally I resorted to Dr. Spock's solution—close the door—but I could still hear her. So I would check once again to make sure I hadn't pinned the diaper to her skin.

Nothing was wrong with her, the pediatrician told us; she would outgrow it. My husband found some newspaper article suggesting the problem was the mother, and though I thought it was nonsense, it left its mark. There was only one time when she stopped crying in apparent response to something I did.

I was holding her, walking around the house with her, wanting to put her back in the crib and go out on the street where I couldn't hear her. Instead I just took her with me, though it was raining. Halfway down the West Village block she became quiet. But her father rounded the corner and asked if I was crazy to have her out in the rain like that. Although the question annoyed me, I wondered if there were some truth in it, if a baby could make you crazy. Or if I were simply unfit to have one, as I sometimes feared.

But I thought motherhood would be good for Poco. She took serious possession of things she considered hers, like a Stop and Shop receipt she found on the floor, carrying them to her crate to guard. I made a point of taking them away from her, to make sure she didn't get overly possessive. My belief that she would like motherhood was perhaps fanciful, however. I was aware that if she needed a C-section she might reject the pups, not realizing that they came from her. That sometimes happens with primaparas, and I was ready to hand-feed the litter if necessary. But I was not prepared to watch a postpartum bitch die.

In that respect human mothers can be considered better at the job because they usually live to do it. I never worried about dying when I gave birth, but I was aware of the risk in dogs. When Poco was pregnant, I had seen an obituary of a lovely bitch in our breed club magazine. The owners didn't spell it out, but you could tell from her young age and the detail about a Basenji foster mother what had happened. Still I hadn't believed I would see Poco panting for her last breath two hours after a Caesarean delivery.

Thirty-five years earlier, the Demerol, the anesthetic, helped me forget pain. But now there were five orphan pups under a heat lamp in the surgery, crying loudly for the milk they would never get. I was crying into the vet's tie as he held my head against his chest. I knew I had to pull myself together and prepare my burden for the trip home.

The vet weighed the puppies, showed me how to tube feed them, and—having determined that they could suck and needed something bigger than a puppy nurser—sent one of the techs out for human bottles and an assortment of nipples. We selected the one with the right flow, then let each one try it. While tubing them would be faster, bottle-feeding was better because it would satisfy their need to suckle, give them some exercise, and provide more contact with their sole caregiver. I was to do this every two hours round the clock.

The departure from the hospital, such a celebrated occasion for new parents and a swaddled baby first exposed to daylight, was more funereal in the evening rain: a small cortege carrying Poco's portable whelping box, the cooler of pups on a latex glove filled with warm water, and a half case of formula. Was I all right, they asked. Yes, I told them, though I hadn't slept or eaten in twenty-four hours.

I wanted to get on the road and play the Brahms *German Requiem*. The forty-five-minute drive would allow me to hear the part that applied, "Denn alles Fleisches ist wie Gras." But in the heavy rain and traffic I couldn't get the tape in right, kept picking up the joyful sections. Besides I had no business risking the lives of five puppies so dearly bought. The trip was therefore quiet, with them sleeping on their artificial mother after their artificial feeding. I kept my mind on the task at hand and the task before me.

·· 2 ··

here were surprises when I got home, though I had carefully readjusted my plans during the hour on the road. There hadn't been any—at least no unpleasant ones— when we brought Jennifer home to the little house on Weehawken Street on a crisp October morning. My husband had set up the crib they wouldn't deliver until the baby was born. Even that ominous precaution hadn't worried me. The nurse we hired for three weeks was ready to feed her while we ate the lunch she'd made for us. The house was clean and welcoming for our new family of three.

Although I'd left the Southport house in good order, it was prepared for both the dead mother and her babies that April evening. There was her water dish in the kitchen, the can of chicken and rice soup on the counter. The 30 × 30 × 18-inch whelping box with foam pad, where Poco had slept for a week, was freshly made up. But it was absurdly large for five rat-size puppies.

I transferred them and the glove from the cooler to their changing box, a smaller one I used when making up the big one, turned on the infrared lamp, and—in the scant half-hour before it was time to feed them—I set about getting everything of Poco's out of sight. I couldn't remove the plywood whelping box, but I turned it on its side to make a counter for all I would need to feed and clean her puppies. I still couldn't stop crying. This was the postpartum depression I escaped with my daughter.

I wasn't busy during the first three weeks of Jennifer's life, and I had planned it that way, as a transition from a life I could manage to one that made me nervous. I wanted to enjoy her and our family status in a relaxed setting, which the nurse provided. By the time she left, the baby was sleeping through most of the night—and not crying, now that I think about it. It might, indeed, have been my fault that she did, my failure to devote those three weeks to her.

With Poco's orphans, however, I needed demanding work to fend off utter despair: I had not been without an adult corgi for twenty years. Normally the first three weeks are the easiest with a litter. The puppies are cared for almost exclusively by the dam, who often doesn't even want to leave them to go out. All you have to do is see that she does, feed her enough for all, change the bedding daily, and keep a close eye on her pups for any signs of illness, chilling, overheating, failure to thrive. Watching them consumes time only because it is fun. By the time the bitch gets tired of them— which she may show by regurgitating food that they immediately devour—you are rested and eager to start the weaning process. Yet I turned down the offer of a foster mother.

Word of my dilemma got around in the corgi world, which I already knew to be very supportive, more so perhaps than the world in general. A breeder in northeastern Connecticut called to say she had a quiet, easy-going bitch who still didn't want to leave her five-week-old puppies. I was welcome to have her nurse Poco's. I received this call on the answering machine, as I could seldom pick up. Before returning it, I carefully considered the offer. Apart from the possibility of infection, which was very real given that my puppies had no maternal antibodies from their mother's first milk and would not get this colostrum from a foster mother, I was not disposed to find a way to avoid the risk. It might have been as simple as bathing the bitch in an antibacterial shampoo.

Tired as I was, with no more than an occasional hour's nap (it took half an hour to feed and clean them, so I had only an hour and a half to eat, go to the bathroom, shower, or sleep after any feeding), I regarded them as *my* puppies after only two days of caring for them. I didn't quite trust my instinct, however, so I called the vet before making the decision, or at least to ask if it was foolhardy, for I had already made it. I thanked my breeder friend and embarked on the job my vet knew I needed.

My sister said she couldn't imagine me nursing puppies. Without inquiring, I took that to mean she didn't consider me very maternal. In truth I had not been with Jennifer; not only did I not breast-feed her, but I let the nurse give her bottles until just before she left. My hope of thus establishing a new and closer relationship with her father during that time was not realized. He was concerned that I didn't want to be with her all the time. I might have been better off busy with my daughter, jumping head-on into the uneasy mothering role; and so, I realize now, might she — just the two of us.

Of necessity it was just me and the puppies. Any visitor posed a risk to their total lack of immunity, and I was not fit company for anybody but them. I rather liked it that way. I realized I'd begun to enjoy feeding them when — instead of setting the clock every two hours, after not even falling asleep on my nearby futon — I began to wait for the first squeal of hunger. It invariably came, and I responded with the bottle. Cleaning them was another matter, not the delicate procedure with a cotton ball described in the books. Even at a few days old, they produced a lot, requiring paper towels and Baggies. I marveled that a bitch could do this so well, with never a stain on the bedding. If these puppies objected to my method, they didn't let on. Except when I waited for them to wake me, they didn't cry at all.

··3··

*O*ur peace had to be interrupted when they were three days old. Nobody looks forward to doing tails and dewclaws, and this time I positively resented the procedure, though it is relatively quick and painless. The dewclaws are snipped out almost bloodlessly, and the tails are tied tightly at the base with rubber bands, which cause them to shrivel and fall off a few days later. A breeder friend from Westchester came over to do the job, and she carefully abided by all the sanitary precautions I spelled out. Even though she had helped me do this with several litters, I found myself responding defensively to any comments she made about how I was raising them. For all her expertise she had never hand-reared a litter. I felt the same resentment I had when Jennifer's father commented on my mothering, a role in which I was now confident.

The puppies fussed for about an hour, as they usually do, but in this case I didn't have to worry about their mother's anxiety. My own was minimal, since I understood what was wrong. After an hour's sound sleep, they were all eager to eat and took more formula than usual. I was so relieved to have the ordeal over that I didn't even try to get any sleep; instead I watched them and began thinking of which ones I liked.

I had done this only mechanically until now, by numbering and feeding them in ascending order of attractiveness, based mainly on markings. The very plain male was first, and two bitches, marked flashily on the head and neck, with long white front stockings rather than socks, were fourth and fifth. I wouldn't have to worry about their testicles descending, and their coats seemed correct. I might keep both. Such a positive thought surprised me. When they began to stir, and before they cried, I warmed the formula, as I was eager to handle and study them.

Again they nursed heartily. But Number Five, the prettiest, didn't feel right when I got to her. She was limp and refused the nipple. I knew enough not to tube feed her until I found out what was wrong. Holding her against my skin under my shirt, I called the emergency clinic, which is in my hospital. After a series of conversations—punctuated by my following the on-call vet's advice and seeing no improvement—I realized the puppy wasn't going to make it. But an emergency vet's job is to save lives, even if it meant subjecting my puppy to an hour's drive, exposing her to very sick animals, and leaving my others for two hours or more. By now she was breathing in gasps. I decided to call my regular vet at home; he had given me the number when I left with my orphans.

He told me what I needed to know: "She's going to die. I'm sorry. Just keep her warm and let her." I could have done that with a latex glove, a towel, and a separate box, except that I couldn't put her down. I wrapped her and the glove in a towel and just walked around with her. It took longer than I thought. Eventually I sat on the milking stool I used to feed them and finally she jerked her head, shuddered, defecated, and that was it. I at least had something to do: put her in a plastic bag in the refrigerator so that she could be posted later. But that didn't take long, as I had the bag ready and a space cleared at the back of the refrigerator where I wouldn't see it.

Then I cried harder and longer than I had at any point after Poco died. I had lost puppies before, including the sole survivor—

on Christmas day—of a difficult whelping botched by an incompetent vet. But I had never been so upset as I was now by the loss of this beautiful little bitch.

There was also a concern about what killed her; if it was an infection, the others were in jeopardy. This anxiety recalled my response to the first time Jennifer got sick, at age two and a half. We had no idea there was anything wrong with her until she went into a seizure as we were all lying on a South Carolina beach. I remarked that she seemed to be moving her head to the rhythm of rock music from a nearby radio. But when I tried to distract her, I couldn't. We quickly carried her back to the cottage; I held her on the stoop while her father went upstairs to get the car keys. As I waited, unable to revive her, I was sure she was going to die.

I didn't cry as we drove to the doctor's office that I had mentally noted on the road when we first got there. And I tried to be composed when we arrived and she was still unconscious. What was wrong, I asked the doctor. The worst thing would be epilepsy, he said. I thought that was pretty bad; I felt so weak I left the examining table and sat down. The nurse noticed and had me stretch out on the bench. Then I heard the verdict when he removed a thermometer, which registered 103 degrees: "It's a febrile convulsion." He found an ear infection, she gradually came around, and I was able to stand up. The rest of our vacation was uneasy, however, like the days following the death of Number Five in Poco's litter.

Mercifully there was no evidence of infection in the autopsy. The possible cause of death was an injury, which made me wonder if I had held her too tight during the tail and dewclaw procedure. I already felt guilty about Poco, who hadn't asked to be bred except when put to the stud. Jennifer hadn't asked to be born either, I told myself often during our troubled life together. Yet I hadn't even noticed she was sick until she had a convulsion. I know that probably nothing I did could have altered the medical course of her or Poco's lives, but I will never be sure about the puppy.

·•4·•

*H*appily the remaining four puppies continued to thrive: they were, in fact, the biggest and most robust I had ever had. And they learned faster. They were eliminating on their own at a week, eating out of individual dishes at two and a half, even though they had to sit down to do it, and drinking out of a water dish a couple of days later, when I abandoned the bottles except at bedtime, a word that finally began to have a meaning. I now fed them four meals a day, and the first would be a good six or seven hours after I turned out the light. Like Jennifer when the nurse left, they were sleeping through the night. But this time *I* had been the nurse.

The period between three and four weeks in all puppies' lives is considered one of "fear imprint" because they are suddenly able to see and hear what is going on around them. Instead of fumbling, as I was with Jennifer, I was carefully letting them hear the radio, look in the refrigerator, watch the shower run, and introducing them to their new quarters, which consisted of a 2 × 4-foot indoor pen with a soft rubber rug-liner for flooring with good traction and newsprint at one end for elimination. Because they didn't seem at all scared, I put them in it before four weeks. The time between cardboard boxes of increasing size and the pen was so

short that they spent only a few days in the whelping box, which—
for me—still held the ghost of their mother, whom they never saw
and maybe never missed. But Jennifer must have missed me during
what might have been a crucial three weeks for her.

I didn't make these comparisons at the time. I was too busy, for
one thing. For another, as the puppies thrived, I consciously
reflected only on the good job I was doing. I didn't feel this way
about Jennifer until she started nursery school; her teacher told me
at our conference to keep on with whatever I was doing because she
was wonderful. My pride was short-lived, however. The kindergarten
teacher asked me how she acted at *home*. It was obvious she was a
problem at school, the same one she attended the year before. Her
father had been out of the picture—or the house—for two years,
and that was one reason I was so proud of whatever I did, if only for
a year. The parenting we planned to share was my sole responsibility.

What I did for the puppies was also exclusively my job. Their
father was less than a ghost, someone they would never know. What
I tried to do for Jennifer began as my part of a joint project born of
mutual love. In both cases I was on leave from teaching. I was given
a year off for the baby because the male chairman of my department thought a semester was insufficient to take proper care of
her; but in January we needed the money and the university
needed me part-time, so I went back. I was more in command of
both my job and my income when I bred Poco: I had accepted an
early retirement buyout, with the intention of teaching one night
class as an adjunct. But I gave myself a year's "sabbatical"—to read,
write, devote full time to the litter. Wise plan, and not dictated by
an employer or a shared income.

I came to wonder, with the puppies, whether I had to be sixty-
five and independent of work or spouse to be a good mother—not
just a "good enough" one, not just a parent, but a mother superior,
the "perfect mother" every woman aspires to become as soon as
she knows she is pregnant with a wanted child.

Fun is what it was now, something I hadn't factored into the ideal of perfect motherhood. Before it was more a need to be right, to know what to do and do it correctly. I didn't believe—and still don't—that good mothering comes naturally to women, that the instinct kicks in when the baby arrives. Yet these very things had happened to me with the puppies, from the moment I stopped setting the clock and let them wake me. Perhaps I missed that opportunity with Jennifer because the nurse was caring for her.

Mothering has to be instinctive with a brood bitch; there are no books to tell her how to do it. She is rather pathetically unaware of what's wrong with her a few weeks after an arranged breeding. She sometimes gets the equivalent of morning sickness, and by five or six weeks into a nine-week gestation, she looks distinctly uncomfortable after she eats. She is puzzled by fetal movement—multiples of what a woman feels.

In first-stage labor she "nests," scratching around in the whelping box, lying down, then scratching some more, as if that still doesn't suit her. The word "nesting" is used in many books, which suggests she knows what she is doing, but surely it's the same behavior exhibited by dogs who simply can't get comfortable. As labor progresses, she may vomit, and I have never read that she does this from pain. When I was having a strong contraction I eyed the bathroom, wanting to go in and be sick. But when it passed, I wasn't in pain, so I didn't.

A whelping bitch never gets a sedative, and she will start to push without being ordered by making repeated efforts to urinate or defecate. Eventually—if she doesn't have uterine inertia as Poco did—she will pass a bubble of amniotic fluid. Licking this seems to give her a taste of what's coming. In an ideal birth, she will do this to the head of the first puppy and tear off the placental sac, freeing it to breathe and stimulating its body in the same way, after which she nurtures them all with exclusive devotion.

··5··

ut this isn't an ideal world. The first puppy may be the biggest, backwards, and out of the sac, a dangerous situation requiring quick delivery by skilled hands. And even then it might be dead. The bitch with inertia is a worse-case scenario. Unable to have hard contractions, she frequently gets an injection of oxytocin, which, women who have been thus induced tell me, is very painful.

It was reassuring that my vet gave it to Poco gradually, via an IV drip, after she was fully dilated. Not only is this easier on the bitch but it avoids the risk of having all the placentas detach at once, too long before she can get the puppies out over a period of several hours. Two hours after the oxytocin, eight hours since her water broke, thirty-six from the last time she ate—with no contractions visible to me or my vet's nurse, who stayed with us from the time Poco was put on the drip—we decided to do a section.

Even if she managed to get one or two pups out in time, it was unlikely she could deliver the five we knew she was carrying. This would result in surgery on a worn-out bitch. I was so confident when my vet wheeled her and her travelling box away that I didn't say good-bye or good luck. I felt the same relief as when the anesthesiologist put me under so they could pull instead of having me push; the next thing I knew I had a baby girl and she was all right.

While Poco was under anesthetic I made a dreary trip in the rain to several fast food places, looking in vain for breakfast at 3:30 in the afternoon. I settled for coffee and a cigarette and rushed back to the good news: five healthy puppies, four girls and a boy. I would have been happier with more males, but I was grateful for their safe delivery.

"Is *she* OK?" I asked the nurse, not being a breeder who would put the puppies' lives over the mother's. Yes, I was told, though the vet was still "working on her." A couple of pups had been way up in the horns of her uterus and hard to get out. Once they were delivered he gave her more anesthetic while he repaired and replaced the uterus, which is removed for a section on a bitch.

When I did see Poco, after looking at the puppies, I don't think she knew me: her eyes were dilated, she was cold, her blood pressure was low, and she was anemic, from the anesthetic and blood loss. With the nurse trying to hold her up, I rubbed her head and neck. Every few minutes the techs took her temperature and drew a couple of drops of blood for a PCV (a hematocrit in humans). Both remained low, despite heating pads and massage.

Eventually we just turned her over periodically, as she wasn't able to sit up. I heard frequent intercom calls for the attending vet, seemingly every time they checked her blood and temperature. When we saw she was bleeding from the uterus, he inserted a needle into her abdomen to see if she was hemorrhaging and needed a transfusion. She wasn't. But my vet's reassurances before he left for a meeting were wearing thin, and I began to worry, especially when there was talk of going in to see what was wrong. I asked if we couldn't let him do it when he returned at six, only half an hour away. Not only had he done the section but he was a board-certified surgeon.

Then she tried to sit up, and I felt better, calling it to the techs' attention. But they had a different take on it. I noticed she was panting, as did they. "Her breathing has changed," they told the attending vet. He listened with a stethoscope, then went away. Within a minute the table was surrounded by at least four techs, two of whom were pulling the top and bottom of her chest from opposite sides of the table. The vet was at her side. "Doesn't sound good," one of the techs told him, and he asked me to leave.

The minute I was in the private passageway between the surgery and the waiting room I began to sob. Poco was dying, and they had sent me out so they could do CPR on her. I went back to "our" room—hers and mine—to be alone with her effects. There weren't many, her box being gone, but there were the newsprint and beach towel on the floor, where I had lain down next to her while she dealt with unknown sensations. Now I sat on the table, where the attending vet finally found me. "She passed on," he said. This was no surprise, but I was annoyed at the euphemism. I later remembered what they told me when they did repeated X-rays while I was in labor: "The baby's twisted around." The baby was a *breech,* and none of my Lamaze techniques would ever get her out. Poco was *dead.*

Coolly, I told him I wanted my vet to do an autopsy. He nodded, and I felt sorry for him as he protested that it wasn't the anemia, it must have been an embolism. I went back with him to the puppies. Did I have another bitch who could nurse them, he asked. Then I broke down. Pointing to them, I cried that they were all I had. I heard my vet paging him on the intercom. I felt especially bad for him, knowing the news he was about to hear.

I wasn't sympathetic with anyone attending Jennifer's birth, including her nervous father, who was clearly relieved when the nurse told him that if I had a second shot of Demerol he would have to leave. I was hostile to the interns who were hurting me so much as they repeatedly turned the baby into a normal birth position. I didn't know they were withholding the truth until later. Even my obstetrician, whom I liked, supported the lie. When the anesthesiologist finally informed me of what she planned to do, I responded with something like "It's about time."

Perhaps it was some thirty-five more years of maturity that made the difference in my response now, or I felt Poco's pain more deeply than my own. What threw me into uncontrollable sobs was my vet's anguish on his return. "I shouldn't have left," he said, putting his arms around me. "You needed me." Then to the techs, who were standing ghost-like against the wall: "And *you* did. I should have been here." Even the next day, after he confirmed an embolism in autopsy, he replied to some question I asked that he had pondered it himself during a sleepless night. Again I cried, knowing he had been awake with me, and for the same reason.

··6··

In the parallels I had drawn between the birth of Poco's litter and that of Jennifer, I was the mother and Poco the baby—until she died. After everyone involved had expressed his or her grief, the shift was sudden. I lifted my head from the vet's chest and managed to stand up. I had started toward the puppies, but one of the techs brought the box to the table. Another brought a scale, formula, syringe, and tube. My vet took over, explaining everything. I was paying close attention, for they were my babies now, my only ones, and mine only.

If April had been the cruelest month for me and Poco, May was uncharacteristically fine, for me and her orphans, my puppies. Despite the poetic showers/flowers sequence, May in southwestern Connecticut tends to be a delayed April, with rain for days on end, what some colleagues and I referred to as suicide weather. Just when classes were over, the only thing we could do with our freedom was stay inside and read student papers. This year I had nothing to keep me in: at four weeks the puppies were physically and emotionally ready to be outside, in a large pen on the open porch or even in a small area of my fenced yard, well away from the street.

Finally I could show off the fruits of my pain and labor. Happily

I disinfected the big pen and set it up on the porch for yet another stage of puppy-rearing. The necessity for such frequent changes in accommodation and venue can be tiresome: no sooner is every-thing in place and working than you have to move on to the next phase. But this time I enjoyed the progress. As soon as I finished the porch pen I unrolled and straightened fifty feet of vinyl-covered rabbit wire with which to partition off an area of the yard for them. Within that was to be a circle of smaller wire designed to protect flowers. After I went back to the clean, dry porch and put down the rug liner, I was ready to bring out the puppies.

My daughter was also about four weeks old when I first took her out in the rain. I don't remember how old she was supposed to be before going out—six weeks? The rule having been broken by a "crazy" mother, I have no recollection of her proper debut in the carriage. What I *do* remember is that I got a lot of unsolicited advice from total strangers—New Yorkers looking out for her wel-fare. Was she warm enough? Shouldn't she have a hat? Should I have that bag of groceries in there with her? This was when I com-bined outings with errands. Going out was usually more trouble than fun, and I couldn't imagine much pleasure in it for an infant.

I did, however, enjoy a strenuous stint building a new accom-modation for Jennifer as a child. On Christmas Eve of her nursery school year—when I was studying six days a week for my Ph.D. orals and teaching a Friday night class on the other—her paternal grandmother died. Whether as a gift she had set aside or a small legacy, there was $100 for Jennifer. In the course of a gloomy Christmas, I decided we could use the money to convert our attic, which had been her father's office, into a cheerful playroom/study where we could be together in a new setting.

Although the project now strikes me as incredibly ambitious, the biggest decision was to take off the time, which was a school vacation after all, even though that didn't affect my need to study. I suggested it to Jennifer, and when she readily agreed to this use of her gift, I went for it. Together we bought—and lugged home—lumber, paint, and fabric.

There had never been a rail by the stairs, so the attic wasn't safe for a child. And despite two small skylights, the whole of it, from floor to ceiling, was a dingy battleship gray. A three-quarter mattress and an old trunk were the only furnishings; my husband had taken his even older desk. I built a bookcase along the stairwell, made a platform for the mattress, painted the walls and ceiling white and the floor a bright yellow. If we didn't get sun from above, I told Jennifer, we would have it on the floor. I used olive on the trunk, yellow on the bookshelves, orange/yellow/olive stripes on the madras bedspread, and orange burlap as hangings to hide storage areas in two corners.

It was a spectacular transformation to my mind, and Jennifer seemed to like it. There was room for her wheel toys, dollhouse, painting materials, and brick-size Legos. The bed was where I studied, with the books I needed at hand on the new shelf. It was a room of our own, and creating it was perhaps the best vacation of my life. But I am not sure how much good it did Jennifer. There was no one to assess the improvement, which was literally and figuratively an interior one. Unless *that* was what I did right when she was in nursery school.

Devising exterior puppy quarters was not like a vacation from other work. It was rather a job I looked forward to because of a predictably pleasant outcome: the public response to little wooly bears of indeterminate breed except to those who knew me as the corgi lady. My puppies always stopped pedestrian traffic and no small number of vehicles at a busy corner in the village of Southport. Although the admiration and questions were time-consuming, especially when I had to be off to teach in the afternoon, they invariably pleased me.

Now, being retired and having lavished my free time as well as my grief on raising the litter well, I was happy to respond. All women may love a baby, but puppies cross the gender gap; men are unashamedly enthralled. And no one, of either sex, presumes to tell you what you should do with them. Instead they ask and marvel. Was that what I wanted as a human mother, praise and admiration? If so, I know now, I wasn't likely to get it. Nobody perceives a mother as an expert because everybody has one whose good and bad points combine to form a personal ideal that isn't you. But when I raised Poco's litter, everyone praised my mothering of her babies.

As a realistic human mother, I was always cynical about people who oohed and ahhed over my baby, saying how adorable she was as an infant. I refused to have the photographer who was cruising the maternity ward take her picture when she looked much like all the other ones—ugly. And the only thing that makes newborn puppies photogenic is being lined up nursing their dam, who invariably looks her best—in full coat and alert: ears up, eyes bright, proud you might say. They themselves are as unattractive at that age as a baby, and I was not the glowing mother when I brought Poco's home.

But by the time of their first outing, I was more inclined to agree that they were cute than I was about Jennifer when I first took her out. She simply seemed to be a bigger baby, until she smiled a couple of weeks later and became uniquely human. The puppies already acted like dogs, standing, sitting, walking, playing. But they weren't yet recognizable as corgis. It was this—the breed itself and my twenty-year involvement with it—that accounted for their uniqueness and my pride rather than a preference for dogs over people, puppies over babies.

*C*ats were what my husband fancied, and he named them after characters in Henry James, but he was catless when we married. We knew there had been a dog at the Weehawken Street house; we could tell by the urine smell under the porch linoleum near the door. I ripped it all up, bleached out the wooden floor, and painted it an olive green to match the shutters and outside steps. Then we met the dog, Muldoon, named for a former girlfriend of her owner. He brought her by to offer her to us in her old home, since he was moving to Texas. We told him we weren't sure; as a new couple we didn't have a child or pet to tie us down.

So Muldoon ended up with a neighbor who would keep her as long as she could—before surrendering her to the ASPCA. I felt this sword of Damocles hanging over her head every time I saw her being walked, and one day I tried to suggest to my husband that we adopt her. I ended up in inarticulate sobs, possibly the first time I had cried in front of him; I realize now how much more natural it seems to cry about dogs than people. He was sympathetic: "Don't worry, we'll just take her," a generous concession for a cat person. The next day we did, a medium-sized brown mutt who appeared to have some whippet in her pedigree.

My husband had never had a dog, and I hadn't since I went to college, when my mother remained the caregiver. But the adoption worked out well, once we got her housetrained. She trained us to let her sleep on the bed, being both affectionate and persistent. She was fun to walk as every dog-loving New Yorker wanted to know what breed she was. "Part whippet, we think," we would tell them. I had hoped we might get a purebred when we were really ready for a dog, a whippet being my choice. But Muldoon came along, lived with us until we split up, then with Jennifer and me until she died at fourteen. She was never a source of discord in our marriage, and she took well to the baby, who was.

A few months after Muldoon died I called the Connecticut Humane Society to find out what they had in the way of moderate size dogs. A beagle mix and a corgi. By the time I got there the beagle mix was gone. I thought the corgi was appealing, but I insisted on reading up on the breed before taking her. I was able to learn very little, the subculture of purebred dogs being almost inaccessible via traditional research techniques. A paragraph here and there had to suffice, and I went back for her late that afternoon.

If Muldoon was fun to walk in New York, Morgan (renamed for a less evil literary character than her original namesake, Reagan) was a showstopper in Southport. That was not my top priority, however, as I had actually wanted the beagle mix, for reasons I could never imagine now. But Jennifer liked Morgan, for one thing, as did the neighborhood kids. I was looking for something new to bond us, as Muldoon had for twelve years, despite our difficulties and her lack of friends.

Most people recognized the breed when we walked her, commenting that you didn't see many corgis. At the time you didn't, at least on the street, but they probably abounded—as they still do—among horse people. Now they rank twenty-sixth in popularity of nearly a hundred and fifty breeds recognized by the American Kennel Club. People who didn't know would ask if Morgan was a cross between a dachshund and a German shepherd. We would explain, then dismiss them as just like New Yorkers. At home we found her smart, affectionate, and humorous, all traits that made for the three-way bonding I sought.

But I was the one intrigued with her breed traits. Like every first-time corgi owner, I thought she fit the standard perfectly. Her foxy face was what most distinguished her to me, and at the other end her neat tail dock; her short little legs were about as far as you could get from those of the whippet I once wanted. But this was to be my breed, I realized, complete with its stubbornness. Morgan had successfully resisted discipline in the eleven months when she was Reagan, and I undertook that task by enrolling us in an obedience class. We worked so hard to please our drill sergeant of a teacher that we finished first in our class. We had become a team.

·· *8* ··

"Team" was the word Jennifer's psychiatrist had used when I expressed anxiety about leaving New York for my new job in Connecticut—away from him and her father. "You'll be a team," he said, and I liked the concept: the two of us in my little Renault, exploring the shoreline, the rolling hills, the rivers and lakes, the New England villages, the farmlands, the college campuses of our new state.

She obediently went along, but she always wanted to take her Raggedy Ann doll and sit in the back seat with her. Once when we set out spontaneously after some errand, she asked if we could go back and get Raggedy; I was so annoyed I told her that better still we would just not go. She didn't seem to mind, but I did. Neither of us knew many people that summer before school started. Why was my company not enough?

I tried another approach with new Raleigh bicycles. In the late afternoons we would take increasingly longer rides along the many scenic little roads around Southport. I named them Route 1, Route 2, and so on, and would enthusiastically ask which route she preferred as we wheeled our bikes onto the street. She was usually eyeing the yard where two little girls about her age lived. "Can they go with us?" she asked. I invited them, but they didn't want to go either. So I took Route 1, the shortest, by myself, and she was in the house alone when I returned. It wasn't even that she had any other company.

The following summer, after a full-time salary that was all mine, I planned a trip to Europe for us. Jennifer, then eight, had been once with her father, who went every year, and he said she enjoyed it. I wanted to give her that pleasure, to go places that appealed to both of us, the team of American womanhood. It was fun during the winter to plot our island itinerary, with lots of boats connecting them. After the Isle of Wight, England, and Norway, Legoland in Jutland, Denmark, was the high point; this was followed by the Hans Christian Andersen museum in Odense, and the Tivoli Gardens in Copenhagen, where I would deliver her to her father. I would then go on more boats to Helsinki, Stockholm, Gotland, and Bornholm.

Little of the trip seemed to excite Jennifer, sometimes for good reason—like London restaurants and museums, where children were conspicuously absent and probably unwanted. But I had expected her to enjoy the cliff beaches on the Isle of Wight, if only because they were like Block Island, where she had vacationed separately with me and her father. She slept through a lot of the spectacular day-long train trip from Bergen to Oslo: snow, mountains, glaciers such as neither of us had ever seen.

I was the enthusiastic one at Legoland, though I hate theme parks; the castles, trains, and restaurants—all made of giant Legos—fascinated me. But Jennifer apparently preferred those in the Weehawken Street attic. Andersen's artifacts were rather gloomy and depressed both of us, but I liked his paper cutouts and still have some of them. Even the Tivoli Gardens, with restaurants where children were more than welcome and the *al fresco* food— from open-faced sandwiches to long red hot dogs—was superb, were not a big hit with her.

Alone in Helsinki, the loneliest city I have ever visited, with drunks on the streets and in the parks early in the morning but very few pedestrians or open restaurants after eight in the evening, I wished for someone, anyone, to share my bafflement with that inaccessible language and city. Anyone but Jennifer.

If it was a mistake to have dragged her everywhere I did, it would have been disastrous to have her there. The one place where I felt comfortable and truly missed her was in the Marimekko store. I used their bold fabrics for clothes of my own and had made several little Marimekkos for her. Not mother-daughter at all; hers were as different in style, color, and design as we were. But despite compliments, I had the impression she didn't like hers. No sense buying her a readymade one in Helsinki.

During my month of travelling without Jennifer, at times when I wished she were there—to enjoy rich pastries at outdoor cafes on Gotland, to be bicycling beside me along the coast of Bornholm—I could nonetheless see how it would really be. Our only chance to be a team was at home.

··9··

This chance inspired my hope that our new corgi would bring us together as a team and take us in new directions. I had never been to a dog show, but after Morgan's stellar performance in her obedience class the instructor advised me to take her to some matches—informal shows—and if she did well, apply to the AKC for permission to compete at its sanctioned shows for a CD (Companion Dog) title. That seemed to me what she already was, but I liked the idea of showing her.

At the matches, however, Morgan didn't act the way she did in class. She would heel and sit, and sometimes come when called, but she invariably broke long sits and downs—that is, she got up. After several such experiences, I decided Morgan would never get a CD in bona fide dog shows.

The first one I went to was entirely by accident: unaware that it was being held on the university grounds, I drove over to my office on a Sunday in June. At first I was rather huffy about paying the modest gate fee, since it was my turf, but I felt a little bad when the man asked, "Don't you want to see the show?"

I drove on up the hill to find the whole campus transformed: dozens of big blue and yellow striped tents, rings and rings of elegant dogs of exotic breeds being gaited or standing like statues.

Along the peripheries were grooming areas with huge French poodles, rope-coated komondorok, tiny papillons, and yes, even corgis, being variously clipped, sprayed, chalked, blow-dried, all in nooses attached to a pole at the end of a rubber-topped table. On the other side of the show area were rows of concessions, selling every kind of dog product imaginable, plus stands with hot and cold human food.

I never went to my office. Thrilled, I rushed home to get Jennifer, Morgan, and the girls across the street. They would love it. They climbed in the car—I really didn't give them any more choice than Morgan—and I gladly paid for four tickets at the gate. The same man was kind enough not to mention that unentered dogs should not be on the grounds. I parked in a well near my office building, and we were suddenly in the midst of over a thousand dogs.

Morgan was a little intimidated, and the pre-adolescent girls were wide-eyed. But they seemed to take it all in at once and need food and drink, which I got them. Thus fortified, they expressed more interest, though it dwindled when we learned the corgis had already been judged. I did, however, meet some fanciers who wanted to know where I got Morgan and told me about their own. A couple of these are friends today.

We left the corgi people, from whom I had learned that dog shows are a good place to buy supplies more reasonably than at pet stores, with a lot more variety. I bought a nicer obedience collar and lead than the one I'd gotten from the class. Maybe I should try again to enter this new world, which I hoped would be even more interesting to Jennifer if Morgan and I were participants.

··*10*··

*M*atch shows are rather tedious, because you don't know how many dogs will be there or when yours will be judged, so you spend the better part of the day waiting for your turn in the ring. For this reason I never took Jennifer; in fact I went to only a couple more because Morgan was determined not to go through the paces she knew so well. I decided instead just to go and observe at a "point show," those where the AKC awards championship points in conformation and "legs" on obedience titles.

The next show I found by design rather than accident, having subscribed to the AKC *Gazette,* which lists upcoming events. This information is curiously absent from local newspapers and magazines, and even with the AKC's listing, you don't know the time your breed will be judged unless you enter. So I went alone to Westchester at 8:30 in the morning, only to discover when I bought a catalog that the corgis weren't on until 2:00.

Still, I was intrigued by this subculture, so full of busy people and dogs at such an hour on a Saturday. I watched Bouviers and bulldogs, chow chows and Chinese cresteds, great Danes and great Pyrenees. As I studied the catalog, I realized why the schedule wasn't available until a week before the show: somebody, the superintendent, had to divide twenty or so rings among more than a hundred breeds and a thousand dogs over about six hours, not counting various levels and classes of obedience. I observed some of those trials and realized Morgan was hopeless.

But I missed her and Jennifer, even when the corgi people began to gather in the grooming area near their ring. A couple of the ones I had talked to before asked after my dog and "daughters." I explained that only one was mine, and this led to exchanges about how many children and corgis they had, as well as to introductions. One woman told me years later that she had gone into dogs on account of her children, but that they never had any interest in shows. I'm glad she didn't tell me then. I needed the illusion that a world I found so fascinating would bring me and Jennifer together in a way our trip abroad had not. Our best moments there were probably when we saw a dog that reminded us of Muldoon.

I liked these people, whose paths I would never have crossed in my job. I also liked their corgis, which most of them were showing themselves. I had never enjoyed a sport or even a hobby. The intricacies of this combination of the two excited me: I had found my way into it naturally, it incorporated my love of dogs and my daughter, and it was a whole new project to learn not only shows but also my breed.

Having given up on obedience trials for Morgan, who was ineligible for breed competition because of her unknown pedigree and—I was already able to see—unpromising even if she were, I began to think about buying a show corgi. Not only did I want to enter that world, but I also wanted "a spare," as the mother in an Anne Tyler novel said about a second child. I would have occasion to remember that when Poco died and the spares were not dogs at all, just a litter of rats who might not live to doghood. I was careful to include Jennifer in the project, which seemed to interest her more than planning our trip to Europe.

At the suggestion of my new friends with corgis, I subscribed to the quarterly magazine of the Pembroke Welsh Corgi Club of America, which I hoped someday to be asked to join. At the time its events were held in the Northeast, within what I would come to regard as easy driving distance.

This year their annual puppy match, at which members exhibited their little show prospects, was in New Jersey, only about a hundred miles from us. I invited the son and daughter of a colleague who was thinking about getting a corgi, packed a picnic lunch, and set off early on a Saturday morning in May. For once I had a car full of enthusiastic passengers, including companions her own age for Jennifer.

I had never seen any corgi puppies, let alone a building full of them, ranging in age from eight weeks to a year, with whole litters set up in little portable pens. Nor had I ever met so many people devoted to the breed. They were all very cordial to us, introducing themselves and their corgis, telling me about the club, and inviting us to lunch, which was an elaborate affair, prepared by the members. The kids were fascinated by the puppies and their antics, especially as they tried to be show dogs; they more often balked than walked in the ring, but the point was for them to have fun. While I was taken by certain ones, I didn't know enough to evaluate them. But I was comfortable with the breeders, who weren't pushing puppies so much as they were simply getting them out, having them seen.

Although the conversation was about corgis and—when we came to it—the food, my introduction of my colleague's children led to some exchanges of occupation. A retired geology professor from Smith, a director of the Baker Institute at Cornell, a cancer researcher for Sloane Kettering, a surgeon, a banker, a lawyer, and an admissions director at Vassar were among these breeders/exhibitors of Pembroke Welsh corgis.

··*11*··

I couldn't help comparing the vocational variety of the corgi group to what I had found in a "Professional Singles" organization whose gatherings I forced myself to attend because I thought I should be doing something about a social and sex life. They had seemed professional at being on the make but often not much else. An otherwise respectable man at one of them told me he felt he had failed if he didn't "score" every time he attended. While he may have overstated the case, that was the underlying premise which made me hate the parties.

Here, among the corgi people, there was an ambience, a genuine warmth, absent from the singles group. I didn't even know whether they were married, single, divorced, or widowed; it didn't matter. I realize only now that it was after I got my first show corgi when I not only stopped trying to meet men but no longer considered those I had met more naturally—at work, through mutual friends, on vacations—a top priority.

The months between Muldoon's death and our adoption of Morgan represented a deliberate delay: I was involved with a man who didn't like dogs. As soon as he admitted to having someone else, besides his estranged wife, I called the Humane Society. Jennifer seemed pleased by that shift of interest and affection, though it was hard to know what she thought of the men in my life.

Her response was at once, or by turns, curious, jealous, competitive. This all seems natural enough in retrospect, but at the time she snooped deviously, catching me in lies I thought it prudent to tell her when she was seven or so. She acted put out to be excluded from a romantic dinner, though I knew she didn't like long restaurant meals. She flirted, too, enough to make me wonder if she might ask whoever it was, behind my back, whether we were going to get married.

I knew I didn't want to marry again. Among other things, if the person had an academic job in another area, I would have to give up mine and make do as an over-qualified adjunct wherever he was; that was one reason I didn't pursue a relationship with someone at Cornell. I also felt Jennifer wouldn't like either a move or a stepfather. She made fun of her stepmother, who was very fond of her. Her father even told me it was "her feeling for and attitude toward Jennifer" that prompted his decision to marry her. And anybody who married me would have to like dogs, corgis in particular, and live with more than one, the way things were developing.

A sexual relationship was awkward in my house because of Jennifer, and it was difficult to stay over at someone else's, what with her and the dog. I suppose I mainly wanted a partner or escort for a social life, which at the time seemed to consist of couples, except, I was discovering, in the corgi world, where what brought us together was our shared love of the breed. Already, at the PWCCA match, I was thinking in a different kind of plural from couples. Most members of this group had come without their domestic partners, if there were any. I like this "uncoupling," felt freed by it, as some women are by celibacy.

··*12*··

*A*t the puppy match I kept going back to an eight-week-old male, plain red and white except for his chest and stockings, not the flashier type I now like. I sought the opinion of the Sloane Kettering researcher who was also a licensed corgi judge and was writing *The Complete Pembroke Welsh Corgi*. She was to become my mentor, and in that role she was as wise, generous, and patient as my doctoral adviser. "He's a pretty baby," she commented about the one I liked. I realized that what she meant was we didn't know how he'd turn out. I said I couldn't get a puppy then anyway because I was going to Oxford in July on a little fellowship from the English Speaking Union. "Don't do anything until you get there," she told me.

What my mentor meant this time required explanation. I should see the English corgis, which at the time were generally better than ours. Many breeders would sell a quality male of five or six months for export to a good American home. I had to decide what bloodlines I liked and write the breeders of my interest. She would lend me the Welsh Corgi League Handbooks she was using for her book: they had show photographs of English Champions and informal advertisements of puppies and young stock. I could keep the books for a week, but she couldn't spare them any longer. In her place I wouldn't have let a relative stranger borrow books I needed for a deadline. I was touched by her trust and arranged to pick them up the next day.

Mainly because Morgan was at home alone, we left the match before it was over; for once I had to persuade Jennifer that we must leave, rather than giving in to her "Can we go now?" We were talking so excitedly on the way back that we completely forgot the lunch, which we all ate in Southport as supper. She told me later that she felt sorry for my colleague's children because they weren't going to get a puppy for a while. "Neither are we," I said, and explained. But she would be in camp for two months—part of our effort to help her make friends—so she wasn't concerned about a short delay.

Since classes were over, I went at the English handbooks like research on another doctorate. Writing letters to the six or eight breeders I finally settled on was another doctoral exercise, as I knew they didn't like to sell to Americans who kept their dogs "in boxes," crates built into the walls of large kennels. It was easy enough to assure them mine lived like the beloved pet she was, but I also had to let them know that I wasn't a big spender looking for a big winner. Unintentionally the story of how I got into corgis was a plus; they were all impressed that I had "rescued" one. My stated purpose—that I wanted a male for show and breeding—was an overstatement I was unaware of until later. But they honored and rewarded my ambition.

··*13*··

ith Jennifer in camp, I was free to travel around England at leisure after the eight-day seminar. But I didn't want to leave Morgan that long with a live-in sitter, as we had Muldoon, and I was eager to get my show dog. So I confined the trip to two weeks. I also went by plane, despite my fear of flying, to ensure his passage on the return trip.

Those two weeks in Oxford were the busiest, boldest, and most varied of my whole life. I slept less than I ever did studying or working or making love or caring for Jennifer. Because it didn't get dark until after ten and was light again before five in the morning, I felt like the Norwegians in Tromsø who sleep a great deal during their totally dark winter, but stay up most of the summer, when the sun doesn't set.

I did the required seminar work of attending lectures on British culture, discussing the topic at cocktail parties, making banquet conversation with eminent scholars. The expected attendance at meals served in the Jesus College refectory was a pleasure—nothing like the college cafeterias I had known. The days' events were usually over before sundown, too soon to go to bed, so we would go to a pub, and when it closed some of us ended up in a dorm room drinking dark beer like undergraduates. It was often close to two A.M. when I got back to my own room.

I was up by six. I needed a good hour before breakfast to concentrate on my corgi project, for which I had a separate notebook from the one I took to the lectures. I called the breeders from a pay phone outside the dorm and kept a page for each one: what I had written her, her response, the questions I wanted to ask and space for their answers, which I wrote down as soon as I hung up. I didn't make any visits until after the seminar, but in those few days I planned to drive to half a dozen kennels bearing the prefixes of top English bloodlines.

This tour I took from "the American house" on the outskirts of Oxford where my cousin and her U.S. Air Force husband lived with their two young children. I didn't expect this new dimension to my already multifaceted trip. I hadn't seen her since she was a little girl and wasn't sure if we would have anything in common besides being in Oxford at the same time. I hadn't been close to my family, nor had I seen them much after I left the South.

But she and I felt an instant rapport when we met for drinks while I was still at Jesus College. She insisted that their huge spare room, with its own sink, would afford me as much privacy as I wanted and that they would enjoy having me. At forty-five, with the under-thirty daughter of my mother's youngest brother, I felt truly comfortable — perhaps for the first time — in the company of blood relatives.

This was a time of many firsts, not the least of which was driving an English car on the "wrong" side of the road. I arranged to rent a Morris Minor, and my cousin and her husband took me to pick it up. My thought was that he would drive it home, where I could practice in their driveway. "You're going to drive," he said, in a way that brooked no argument, and then got into the passenger seat. He gave me one simple but invaluable piece of advice: the person on the left always has the right of way. Though I was often confused by road signs, intersections, and traffic patterns on roundabouts, I knew what to do and boldly did it. With amazing confidence I headed off to the first breeder.

They were all warm and hospitable: I was served everything from "elevenses" to a plowman's lunch to tea and cake when I visited their dogs. After seeing all but the last one, I was most taken with a litter of four 12-week-old bitches, quite pretty and just my type. I was aware that despite my preference for a male, I was lucky to be offered one of these females, who were also from the bloodlines I liked.

But the next day I went to the breeder who developed those bloodlines. That's where I found Paddington Bear, a very correct fifteen-month-old with a foxy face, dark brown eyes, and a sweet expression. He would do anything for his breeder: stand on an examining table, gait smartly on a loose lead, strike a good pose when she baited him. He was even a proven stud, with the puppies due in about a week; I saw the bitch, heavy in whelp, sitting a bit mournfully with her load.

But Paddington was shy, she told me, though he had several nice placements at specialty shows exclusively for corgis. He didn't want to look me in the eye at first; then he did and I petted him. On her instruction I myself gaited him and put him on the table. She seemed satisfied that I would do right by him and I readily agreed to the modest price she quoted.

I left him there for the remaining two days of my stay. My cousin and I celebrated with a lot of beer and a long talk about the problems of being women and mothers. Neither of us was comfortable in the role, but I had almost forgotten. It seemed like the first time I had even thought about Jennifer since I left, but I must have written her. It was definitely the first time I had engaged in such a conversation, one that had a permanent impact, like the discussions in those "consciousness-raising groups" I had spurned as a wife and mother.

··*14*··

y two weeks in Oxford were an interlude that marked a
pivotal point in my life. In some ways it was a last fling
as a student with time and energy to get the work done,
party, and pursue private interests. In others it was a conquest of
phobias—transatlantic planes, right-handed cars, life without a
man—to get what I needed. In still another it was an unexpected
return to my family. And it was a new commitment, to Paddington,
his breeder, and corgis.

I wasn't reflecting on this as I took the bus from Oxford to Chol-
sey, where the breeder picked me up to deliver Paddington and me
to Heathrow. Nor was I worrying about the flight. I was only concerned that he not be too scared. And I was grateful to his breeder
for starting me on a new life. It would never be like hers, I realized
when I treated her to lunch at the airport; I had started too late. Her
mother had also been in dogs, English cockers, and she had been a
dog person all her life, with a pet corgi from childhood. She was the
only one of the English breeders I met who made her modest living
that way. She was close to sixty and ran her kennel with the paid help
of one dedicated young woman. I didn't envy her this awesome
responsibility, but I greatly admired her commitment.

Such a smart woman had done without higher education, a

secure job, marriage, children—all the goals I had pursued and attained—to spend her life breeding, exhibiting, and caring for corgis, a hobby I was taking up in middle age. She was known and respected throughout the English-speaking world for the blood-lines she had developed in the course of nearly forty years. Not only were her corgis sound and true to type, but they were largely free of serious faults we would see after she, and her line with her, died: fluffy coats, incorrect bites, undescended testicles. And she was highly regarded as a judge, both in the British Isles and abroad. These judging assignments, in the United States and Canada, Australia and New Zealand, South Africa and Zimbabwe, were her only vacations, paid for by the national corgi clubs that held the shows.

I reflected at the time on the difference in our lives: I would have chosen the career I did, but would I have married and had a child? How had she not needed to do that? Why did I? Had I simply felt the social imperative? I could see how maternal she was with her dogs—not only Paddington, who was so devoted to his "mum," but also a bitch she had hand-raised, Patience, who was as outgoing as he was shy. I even questioned my choice of a profession that demanded a doctorate but paid so little. Accustomed to considering myself poor, I had thought a purebred show dog was beyond my means as a single mother. Having learned that he was not, however, I was grateful for my academic schedule, which allowed me to do a lot of work at home, with my dogs as well as my daughter. It was a point I had successfully emphasized with Paddington's breeder.

As I look back now on buying him and meeting her (both of whom would be dead ten years later), I realize that before I was forty years in my job I was burned out. But not her. She was delighted with Paddington's puppies, she wrote enthusiastically, at the beginning of a correspondence that lasted the rest of her life, though there were six males and one female, "a bit of a blow." The male she kept produced as well for her as his sire did for me in the United States.

Paddington's breeder didn't give up until she was terminally ill and essentially alone. Her faithful kennel girl had married, leaving her with only temporary staff. Her best friend let her down when asked to serve as her next-of-kin. Fortunately an American breeder, a happy, well-to-do wife and mother whose children were grown, simply took off a couple of months to ease things for her English mentor: be with her in the hospital, get her affairs in order, and see that her corgis were properly cared for. But a special treat on one of her last good days—taking her home to see the dogs and some new puppies—was a reality check for all concerned. Dying, she had no interest in them.

I couldn't begin to understand her despair at the time, nor can I now. But I felt a hint of it a few years ago when I had emergency surgery for a herniated disk. In a daze of pain and Percocet I made the necessary arrangements about my job, my dogs, and my transportation to the hospital. I was actually glad, the night before I went, that the dogs were at the vet's and I didn't have to feed them or let them out.

But I had wanted them desperately—just to be on my bed—after I called Jennifer that same night to inform her of my first serious surgery. She asked if she could do anything but didn't offer to help on the day I was scheduled to come home, though this was what I told her I needed.

··*15*··

*T*hese events were in an unknown future when I claimed Paddington's crate from customs at Kennedy. He looked very alert, though he was not eager to come out and walk on a leash. The friend who stayed with Morgan met us, and only when we got home did Paddington urinate, for the first time in more than eighteen hours.

He seemed to relax a bit when he saw Morgan; there was a trust that didn't yet extend to me. I was glad Jennifer was at camp, as she would have been disappointed on at least two counts: he wasn't a little puppy and he would be afraid of her. I put his crate, with some of his mum's smells on it, in my bedroom. But I left it open in case he wanted to get on the bed with me and Morgan. In the middle of the night he did, but he was back in the crate by daylight.

My mentor suggested I shouldn't show him until I felt he was ready, and added that she was judging corgis at a show in Danbury in late August. As if *I* were ready. When I took him to some matches, I found out how much practice we both needed. He was scared of men, hats, wind, noise, and flapping tents, but I got him used to them in my hapless way. And I studied the formal routine at the Danbury show, where I went without him. With a pencil and legal pad, I noted how exhibitors came into the ring, where they stood, which way they went around, how they gaited their dogs individually, what they did with them on the table, where they went when they were in or out of the ribbons. I still have those diagrams—not that I have anyone to benefit from them.

I didn't take Paddington to meet Jennifer's camp bus either. She asked why, and I told her I thought all the kids would frighten him, that he was shy. For some reason this seemed to appeal to her; perhaps she felt shy herself, as I have and probably everybody has. He ran upstairs and under the bed when we got home. She didn't pursue him, but she always knew where he was. Finally, out in the yard, he came up behind her and sniffed her jeans. She said she was thrilled.

But the idea of dog shows still did not interest Jennifer. She loved him and Morgan as pets who were very different in temperament, but that was it—which was all I could reasonably expect. I had decided Paddington could make his debut at the National Specialty in September, about four hours away in Pennsylvania, and I knew from experience she wouldn't want to spend eight hours in a car with me for any reason. The show was a weekend affair, held on the grounds of the motel where the exhibitors stayed, so I got a sitter for her and Morgan.

I had a good time. It was a very sociable occasion—not a place for children—with people parties and dinners every night for corgi fanciers from all over the country. Paddington seemed singularly at ease among so many of his own breed. I thought at the time that he knew they were corgis, and he probably did, but my reasoning was off. Only recently did it dawn on me that they can't know what they look like. Obviously, it takes a lot more than a show dog and a National Specialty to make a dog person; possibly you have to be born one, like Paddington's breeder.

Her dog—my dog—did win his fifteen-to-eighteen-month sweepstakes class in a non-regular competition for young dogs, with the entry proceeds divided among the winners. But he was out of the ribbons in the regular Open dog class. What I liked then and do now about specialty shows, national or regional, is that people are looking at and admiring the dogs themselves, not just winners. Paddington received his first stud inquiry from a man who told me from ringside how nice he was.

I was abysmally ignorant of stud work, assuming that you just put them together and they "did it" like street dogs. I didn't even realize what was going on when I was trying to get some pictures of Paddington in a remote area of the show site, against a stockade fence that concealed garbage cans. There, behind the fence, were two people with two corgis who were panting and slobbering over each other. I sensed it was something private and left, but I didn't recognize it as a canine singles "score."

I mentioned it at our particularly festive dinner table that night. One somewhat sober breeder, a male, said he thought he knew the case I was talking about: the bitch was ready to be bred, and the stud was at the show, so their owners mated them there. He seemed apologetic, as if the breeding had offended my sensibilities. I asked why they didn't do it in the motel room. "It's kind of messy," he replied, without elaboration. I learned then, without yet realizing I had learned anything, that people's attitudes toward the mating of dogs are as complex as responses to Rorschach tests.

··16··

When I reported to Jennifer that a man with a female named Lady Hope wanted to mate her to Paddington she was excited. She probably thought of the "marriage" as romantic, but she asked some guarded questions about when and where it would take place. I explained that the bitch always came to the dog's home, where he was more at ease, adding a feminist apology for these priorities. That, apparently, was not what concerned her: she didn't want to see it. OK, I said, she didn't have to look.

I didn't know then that you need someone experienced to help mate corgis, unless—as I did with Pesto—you devise a mating procedure whereby you hold the bitch in such a way that the dog can mount and penetrate her and you are able to have your hands on them both during the "tie," which can last anywhere from five to forty-five minutes. This phenomenon is caused by a gross enlargement of a gland at the base of the dog's penis during intromission; he and the bitch are literally tied until it subsides and they separate.

Again, from a feminist perspective—having seen how large this bulb gets during an "outside tie" when you hold them together until the dog has fully ejaculated or during an artificial insemination when you can't breed them naturally—I felt sorry for maiden bitches who didn't even want to be touched inside, let alone invaded by something the size of a golf ball. If Jennifer was instinctively repelled, she didn't know the half of it.

Another thing about stud work I learned was the flexibility it requires. This is not my strong suit, I realized with Jennifer: mothers are always being *interrupted,* well-laid plans go oft awry. It was only after I got tenure that I dared to miss a class and get behind in the syllabus if she was sick. Before that, I engaged an older woman who could stay with her, though I felt she might have preferred me. Your dog and someone else's bitch probably don't care who mates them, but it is your obligation to the bitch owner.

This bitch is due in season some month, and you book her for him, but she might be early or late. After she comes to you, she might or might not be ready to breed on the tenth or twelfth day of her season; and even if she is, your dog might not necessarily oblige. So you take her to the vet for a series of vaginal smears, which can't pinpoint ovulation until after it occurs. And the bitch may have traveled all the way from San Francisco, with the airfare exceeding the stud fee. Or one bitch may be a month late and another a month early, so that they arrive at the same time. Worse than the logistics of keeping them apart from each other and the dog, your stud may appear to fall for the first one and have no interest in the second. He can also refuse to let you do an artificial insemination. Much to worry about.

Many years later I realized this need for flexibility as a bitch owner during what would be Poco's fatal breeding. Even though I was retired, I didn't plan to spend eight days in an Ithaca motel while she and the stud did nothing. They met on Valentine's Day and were apparently quite interested in each other. She was "standing," that is, she stood firmly and tilted her vulva upwards to invite the male. He mounted her but nothing more. Not ready, we decided, and I took her back to the motel.

As the days passed, with Poco staying in the stud owner's kennel, she became increasingly flirtatious, but her Valentine "lost interest entirely," the owner said. He appeared to be taking the matter personally, and I was flexing my mind about another stud at her next season, worrying about her having a first litter at four and a half, wondering if I could still get the Maine cottage I usually booked for June since I wouldn't have young puppies then.

But before giving up I suggested we get a vaginal smear done on Poco. The stud owner and his wife took the dog along to try an artificial insemination at the vet's if she was still in estrus, the ideal time for a successful mating. (The word literally means "frenzy.") She was, but the vet couldn't ejaculate the dog. "He's impotent," the owner moaned, "couldn't even get an erection." I told him something similar had happened with Paddington and Lady Hope, but nothing I said consoled this man, who had successfully mated corgis for some thirty years.

His wife thought it was worth one more try, but he refused to go. So I went with her and the dogs, who had been kept apart. I sat down on the floor of the vet's examining room, holding Poco between my legs with her rear toward the stud, the method I developed for single-handler matings. He flew over to mount her, and the vet, also on the floor, was quick enough with his collection cup to get a couple of cc's of the sperm-rich fraction of the ejaculate, which he examined under a microscope and found good. After he inserted it into her, I kept her upside down with her vulva elevated for ten minutes. Some honeymoon. If I hadn't done stud work with several males and a lot more bitches, I would have been appalled. Given the outcome, I am. Either way, I felt bad about Poco's and my special trip together.

··*17*··

espite this special trip, I wouldn't say Poco was my best friend—then or ever—but I would say a woman's daughter is seldom that, despite Jennifer's psychiatrist's ideal of "a team." Since she lacked friends her own age—a problem she wouldn't admit, let alone discuss—it was hard to make her mine. Nor was I able to help her by arranging with other mothers for their daughters to come over after school, as I did until she was about eight. By then girls made their own play dates.

As long as Jennifer was brooding in her room anyway, I asked her to help with the grocery shopping and laundry, which we had to do at a laundromat. These chores, she claimed, prevented her from being with friends, so we were in a vicious circle not conducive to a mother-daughter friendship. We were more like an old couple who blamed each other for whatever went wrong.

Jennifer perceived her problem as being the only child of divorced parents. Yet my niece—for all my sister's better mothering skills, for her closer relationship with our mother—decided at about twelve, when her parents split up and her father married another woman, that she wanted to live with them. In the process she left her younger brother and whatever friends she had in her first home. My sister had no choice but to deal with this rejection.

And cling to her canine friend, a Dalmatian bitch with a progressive myelopathy that indicated euthanasia.

Even if Poco wasn't my best friend, when I think about what I did to a loyal bitch, even unwittingly, I believe that nothing I ever did to Jennifer—out of ineptitude or frustration—was as unforgivable. She at least had the choice of a child of parents who both wanted her, like my niece. In addition there was the option of boarding school, if she didn't choose to live with either of us. Poco had no alternatives, nor did she complain.

The profundity of this realization has come to me only now. Your daughter, her father, her psychiatrist, your psychiatrist, your mother may variously tell you what you have done, are doing, can do wrong; what you could have done, should be doing right. But your bitch will do what you ask. Because you are doing the best you can for her, and she doesn't protest, no one feels obliged to intervene. What becomes of her is your exclusive and awesome responsibility.

Of course there are veterinarians, humane societies, canine control officers, rescue organizations, dog trainers, behaviorists, theorists, and breed specialists interested primarily in the welfare of dogs. But your dog can't benefit from their care unless you seek it. She can't even get into the pound unless you let her. When you conscientiously abide by the experts' advice, you do so with the consent of your dog, because she has no choice. If she dies delivering puppies that you asked her to have, your obligation to them— her final gift to you—is immeasurable.

So too is the obligation of the professional caregiver you have chosen for her. When Poco's daughter Psallenda turned a year, I scheduled an appointment with our vet to do preliminary X-rays of her hips for genetic screening. This has to be done under anesthesia, a slight risk that entails signing a release. I had never worried about it with this vet, but I called him, ostensibly to make sure he also had time to clean her teeth. Buoyed by the gratitude I had felt on the first anniversary of Psallenda's birth and Poco's death, I made a darkly humorous comment: "If anything happens to her, I want you to have a vial of morphine ready." When he didn't say anything, I added, "For me." I was stunned by his sober response: "For me too."

I know human doctors feel bad when they lose patients, and they would be inhumane if they didn't say so to the survivors. But the bond between a compassionate veterinarian and a conscientious client is incomparable to that between physicians and people. The difference, I believe, is due to a shared love of the dog. The same rules don't apply; feeling on both sides can be and is expressed, even a year after the loss.

No doctor or psychiatrist ever put his arms around me when I cried, nor did Jennifer's psychiatrist seem to understand my concern the way my vet does. The physician attending both of my parents when they died, a neighbor for many years, didn't call me or my sister; he simply told the relatives who were there and let them do it. This distance surrounding members of the medical profession might not strike you as odd unless you have a vet who will get close, and a dog to bring you together in life and death.

Or unless you are lucky enough to have had a physician who will communicate in the same way. When I met the neurosurgeon scheduled to perform my diskectomy, it was in his office because I couldn't check into the hospital immediately. I had to get the dogs boarded.

This surgeon walked in, and his first question was "What kind of dogs is it you have to take care of?" I told him. He smiled broadly in that special way of people who share a love of corgis. "I don't believe it. We have had three of them," he went on in his crisp Pakistani accent. My sciatic nerve was no less inflamed on his examination, but the few minutes of our corgi talk remain a pleasant, pain-free memory.

··*18*··

I consulted my corgis' caregiver when I had everything ready for the transfer of Poco's orphans to the porch and yard at four weeks. Although I felt they were ready temperamentally, I wanted to be sure it was medically safe. "Yes," he said after I described the set-up. "It'll be good for all of you." I had forgotten how much I enjoyed sitting in the spring sun; in fact I hadn't even remembered it was spring those weeks I was nursing the litter.

I didn't get any sun the first day I put the puppies on the porch; none of us stayed outside very long. They took their first look at daylight, the outdoors, trees, the street, people, traffic, and they were sore afraid. As with any procedure you've decided is all right (or necessary) for puppies, you carry on as if whatever you do was what you intended. Seeing them all huddled in the corner of the porch pen close to where I sat reassuring them, I moved to the other side, closer to the street, where they followed me, casting fearful glances beyond me.

After a few minutes I quickly got their food, which I had already prepared. They knew what to do with that and gobbled it down. Counting on reflexes, I immediately moved them to the circular wire pen in the grass, where they did their business in a hurry, then ran over to me. At this point their first audience was gathering, but

I shushed any comments and put the puppies back on the porch. I sat briefly with them on each side of the pen, then took them two-by-two back inside, as if we'd had our picnic and it was naptime. They slept contentedly, while I fretted that their debut had been aborted.

In part I felt cheated of the applause their admirers were eager to provide. But I was more deeply concerned that the absence of their mother was the reason for their fear. She would have been running up to the picket fence for affection and they would have seen that it was safe. Was my mothering still inadequate? I couldn't forget the accusation of being crazy when I first took Jennifer out, or the uneasy sense that maybe I was. But fortunately I could remember my vet's encouragement about the puppies' first outing being good for all of us.

I've admitted to no recollection of the first time I took my daughter outdoors in the carriage. But I recall the affect. For one thing, it was a physically awkward experience; you don't practice pushing an empty baby carriage along the sidewalks of New York, up and down curbs, across treacherous streets. But once the baby was in it, I realized how dangerous a misstep could be, especially with her father worrying that I might make one. There was nothing to show off, since only her face was exposed and barely visible under the hood of the carriage, which was no showy English pram, just a cheap port-a-crib on wheels that I could easily carry up the outside stairs to our house.

I believe we simply walked around the block: Weehawken to Christopher to West to Tenth to Weehawken again. Since our house extended the short distance from Weehawken to West Street anyway, we might just as well have pushed the carriage from the front to the back of the house a few times. But I distinctly remember where I took Jennifer when I first went out alone with her: to an open pier across West Street that had formerly served Norwegian America Lines.

The pier was a favorite haunt of mine: a huge open space jutting into the Hudson River that sun-lovers had quickly adopted as a tar beach. It was never crowded or noisy; we were adults quietly catching rays, reading, having lunch, or just gazing at the water. No one took particular notice of my wheeling a baby carriage out there on a fine Indian summer day in November. Jennifer was quiet, and if she had started to cry, I would have left. I wished at the time, and I did again when I anticipated a summer outdoors with my puppies, that my first trip to the pier with her hadn't been the last. Sharing that peace with my daughter might have established a silent bond. But by late spring she was in a stroller, which wouldn't work in the setting I found so restful.

Where a baby would have been welcome at any age, any time of the year, any day of the week was Washington Square Park. I went once, just to prove my prejudice against "park mothers." I was alone because Jennifer's father didn't think it was a place for men, and in truth it wasn't. I picked a bench at some distance from the playground, which was surrounded with carriages whose occupants were not yet able to play. I had a book, but at first I just leaned my head back in the sun shining through leafless trees. "Ohh, how old is yours?" asked a woman strolling by with hers. I answered that she was "about eight weeks," then felt obliged to return the question. "Seven weeks today," she said, and sat down. After some short exchanges about weight and food intake, I said it was time for Jennifer's nap, which she was already taking, and left.

I was, I realize now, hypersensitive about conversation with "other mothers": well-intentioned friends had regaled me with all the things that could go wrong in childbirth. I bit my tongue to keep from doing the same thing after my breech. But I have never failed to warn would-be breeders about the dangers of whelping. The books usually describe the process, invoke the wisdom of "Mother Nature," list signs of trouble. None tell you your bitch may be alive one minute and dead the next. My mentor did, though;

long before I knew her a bitch carrying ten puppies had died in her arms. I didn't forget this extreme example.

On reflection I can see this pre- and post-natal talk among mothers as something they simply liked or needed, without reference to the welfare of babies. I didn't—not in the way I needed to know how I could best help a brood bitch through a safe delivery of healthy puppies. Her being my dependent, even as she was in the process of giving birth to a litter dependent on her, complicated my maternal obligation in any given breeding. Poco's case compounded it: I lost my dependent, but I gained hers. It was too personal to share with anyone except them, her babies, before they were ready to participate.

That, I see now, was what I wanted with Jennifer while she was just a baby: a private pleasure that I would share only with her father until she herself was able to enjoy socializing. I didn't have any age in mind, as I did with the puppies, because I didn't know. But it seemed to me that friends and relatives who insisted on holding or feeding a two-month-old baby were, like the park mothers, just doing something they liked. Who could say about Jennifer? I could about her father: he wanted to show her off.

My disappointment that the puppies didn't let me show them off the first day I put them out made me understand my husband's eagerness to do it with Jennifer, who didn't object. And my three weeks doing Poco's job made me wonder if I had missed an essential privacy with my daughter when I let the nurse take care of her. Or if *she* had. Nursing those puppies was a humbling as well as an enlightening experience. At the crossroad where I found myself— they were ready to be outside and they didn't want to—it was also a disquieting reminder of the incompetence I felt with my daughter.

··*19*··

I woke earlier than usual the day after I took the puppies out, a bright and sunny new one. But the old worry surfaced and kept me in bed a little longer: should I try them again today or wait? They saw I was awake and clamored at the end of the pen for my attention. "Yes, we'll go out," I told them. "You'll have breakfast on the porch." I lined up the four bowls of food outside the pen, on the street side. As I hoped, they waited there, despite my presence on the "safe" side.

I didn't have much time to congratulate myself while they ate, and indeed I didn't have much reason—it was a pretty basic maneuver. Encouraged, however, I whisked them into the pen on the grass, then took the dishes inside. They were whining at the edges when I went back out with Baggies to pick up their stools. Not finding any, I suspected the problem: they didn't want to soil their new quarters. This is a preference that puppies—corgis anyway—develop at a very early age; even indoors they will go to the very edges of the pen, often managing to get the stool outside it, beyond the newsprint. Now, with so much grass around them, they wanted to use it.

Esa-Pekka, the biggest and boldest, was the first one I put into the main yard. He eventually did his business, but first he almost strode about, sniffing mainly, while his sisters watched him, not me. As soon as I got them out, I positioned myself between them and the picket fence to keep them at a safe distance. The bitches followed the male in the beginning; all chose a toilet area near his. Then they wandered in their own directions, none toward me. I was enchanted. Was this what they wanted yesterday, or had they progressed that much overnight? I kept my back to the street, hoping that no one would interrupt my private pleasure. I had it now—what I missed with Jennifer.

I hadn't expected to use the large enclosure so soon, but the unrolled rabbit wire and stakes were at the ready and the little circular pen was obsolete. Quickly, before anyone could distract us, I gathered my brood and put them back on the porch, where they watched me intently as I began work on the partitions. It went slowly, because by then pedestrians were doing double takes and noticing the puppies. For their part, they began to look with interest at these objects of my attention. Although I was proud of them, what I most cherished were those moments I shared only with them when they ventured into the big yard.

I spent several hours installing the new wire, which would keep the puppies a good six feet from the picket fence in front and altogether out of the back yard. While I worked they slept, lying apart rather than huddled. They didn't seem to need the only canine warmth or comfort they had known. Fleetingly I myself felt—for the first time—that I didn't need Poco.

I was aware people would ask after her. The neighbors knew, of course, but casual admirers would notice her absence. What I didn't expect was a plural: "Where are the others?" Poco's grandfather, Pesto, had died the previous year at eleven. In order to explain about her, I quickly dismissed his death, which was in fact what I myself had done, to make room for another loss. Now they both hit me at once, while I tailored the yard to all I had left: the wooly pups asleep on the porch. By the time I finished and went inside to prepare their lunch, I was crying.

But "all I had left" heard the sound of stainless steel bowls and eagerly lined up at the edge of the pen where they knew I would put them. Now I was as happy as I had been sad five minutes before. It wasn't simply that new life made up for lost life, if it was that at all. It was my babies so trustfully awaiting my nurture. I would be doing this for any puppies their age, but I had never established such exclusive trust from birth. Not even with Jennifer, especially not with her.

If the puppies were grateful for my mothering, they were also delighted with the freedom I gave them in the yard. That I couldn't have done with Pesto and Poco alive. They had their fence friends and would have resented being confined to the back yard. Pesto didn't like puppies, probably because they invariably tried to nurse on his penis. And a lot of mothers—I would never know about Poco—are tired of them after about four weeks. I took some pleasure in the fact that now everything was for my puppies—the house, the porch, the yard, me: I was exclusively committed to them.

··*20*··

otal commitment, was that it? Was good mothering possible only under these circumstances? I had always imagined marriage would be that, not to the man himself but to the union. I hadn't planned to finish my doctorate once I got married, because I hoped to teach only part-time and devote myself primarily to an ideal nuclear family. It was a goal I believed within my grasp as a modern educated wife and mother.

When we expanded to a family, I hoped to be the kind of mother who could combine caring for our daughter with sustaining a good marriage, managing our household, and hanging on to my profession. If my ideal of family life was foolishly romantic, it was at the same time too practical: everything was a job I could handle. There was no involuntary commitment of the kind I would have to Poco's puppies.

Teaching and working on my doctorate were serious commitments on my part until I got married because—having taught full-time for five years—I recognized the limitations of part-time jobs: only freshman composition and introduction to literature, to students who often had little interest in either.

Once I decided I had to at least start on a Ph.D., I chose Columbia; if I was going to do all that work it might as well be at an Ivy

League university. My first hurdle was their qualifying exam for M.A. credits from somewhere else. Well after six P.M. I took the last sheet out of my barely portable Remington and delivered all of them to the patient department chair, a woman.

This middle-aged, unmarried scholar's dedication impressed me, and her recommendation for my first job in the New York area inspired a sense of obligation to both the degree and the profession. What got in the way were love affairs, to which I can't honestly say I was committed, since they tended to be of short duration. Although I always got my work done, I felt shabby about my priorities—until the lover was my chairman at the new job, the man I would eventually marry.

What first attracted me to him was his respect for my work. He arranged for the university to pay my Columbia tuition as an incentive for me to continue taking courses, and he recommended me to a publisher for editing an anthology. I embarked on all this, and even completed it within a couple of years. The classes at Columbia were easy in that neither attendance nor exams were required; you showed what you knew at your orals, after the course work was completed. The anthology—being largely cut and paste—was not as demanding as a scholarly book, but it involved a contract commitment and a deadline.

Shortly before I finished the book, I turned twenty-nine and was counting both the years and the number of lovers: how many was too many and when would I settle down? My professional résumé looked good, but what about my life? My future husband's approach was to the point when he asked whether I planned to get married. I mentioned the lover problem, for which I was seeing a psychiatrist. In the same conversation I found myself telling him I wanted a daughter—in wedlock. So did he, though he was still married to his estranged wife. After that, things got personal. He was older, but good-humored and affectionate. His mature warmth was what I wanted after the hot young lovers I perceived as part of the glamour of New York.

There were suddenly many commitments, like the figs on a full tree that Sylvia Plath—my age—used in *The Bell Jar* as a metaphor for the many exclusive life choices before her as an intelligent, ambitious young woman. I could do it by being the whole tree, not any individual fig; I wouldn't be a full-time teacher, a full-time student, a full-time wife, or a full-time mother. Yet I was each by turns. There were times and occasions—from a few weeks to a year, from deadlines to crises—when I was primarily committed to my daughter, husband, degree, or job, whether I or anyone else liked it or not. But I was never committed exclusively, as I was to my orphan puppies.

··*21*··

One primary commitment was to Jennifer, and it was not unlike my round-the-clock vigil with the puppies. Already uneasy about the future of our marriage, I was diligently pursuing my doctorate and had scheduled the required exam in Old English for a Monday morning, figuring I could practice some last-minute translations over the weekend when her father could help with her. But she began to look sick while I had her in the supermarket on Friday afternoon; I hurried home, and the minute I got there she vomited all over the kitchen. Before I could clean up, she went into convulsions. Knowing what it was, as I hadn't the first time, didn't make it easier to deal with, and doing so alone made it harder.

The pediatrician must have recommended conservative treatment, because we just kept her in bed and gave her fluids on Saturday. I worked on "The Battle of Malden." But she had another seizure on Sunday, and the doctor on call actually came to the house. She was still unconscious when he got there, so he stayed until she regained consciousness. But his advice—to put her in a tub of cold water and really cool down her body—was unsound, as my psychiatrist later explained: doing this made her shiver, which caused her temperature to go up. Consequently she went into a convulsion while we had her in the tub. At this point we got through to her pediatrician, who said we should take her to the emergency room at Mt. Sinai for a spinal tap, to rule out meningitis.

After a couple of hours there, she seemed fine; the attending doctor found her so alert and responsive that he couldn't justify putting her through the spinal tap. But we should keep her cool with alcohol rubs through the night. I was so relieved by his decision that I didn't mind this last interference with my study plans. Nor—being her mother—did I consider asking her father to spell me, though he taught in the evenings and didn't have an exam at nine A.M.

I settled in with Jennifer; the thermometer, alcohol, and *Beowulf* were on the floor between my cot and her bed. I had, after all, done all-nighters in college. But this was different. What kept me awake was not my procrastination but a calling I didn't question. Except for the exam, I might have set a clock, as I first did with the puppies. As with them, however, I suspect I wouldn't have slept.

By morning her fever had been normal for several hours. The Old English exam was feasible, since both my husband and I were comfortable with his watching her while I was gone. I showered, had breakfast, and got on the subway, no more worried than I had been driving up the West Side highway three years earlier to give birth to the daughter I had seen through this crisis.

My successful exam was a comparatively minor achievement. To be sure, staying up all night with a sick child is something few mothers have not done. But in the context of other commitments—faltering like my marriage or progressing like my doctorate—it was a memorable event for me, one Jennifer would not recall.

··*22*··

*I*n the brutal world of the indigent working mother, such a "sacrifice" as a night watch over a feverish daughter doesn't merit the name, nor can her four sons remember her final act in their behalf: all five are dead. I knew the woman by sight as a member of the university custodial staff who seemed to work the night and weekend shifts. She always looked tired and sometimes pregnant, but she brightened up when I was training a puppy in the corridor she was trying to clean on a Saturday afternoon. She didn't speak English, nor—I am sure—did she want to ask what breed of dog it was. She merely responded with affection to a little thing that was actually in her way. The puppy was probably Poco, and the baby she was carrying her youngest son, Pedro.

They were all killed by an Amtrak express train as they were walking along the tracks from Bridgeport to Fairfield, most likely as the shortest, surest way to get somewhere without wheels or money. The children's backpacks contained toys, school-books, coloring books, and personal belongings—the same as a more privileged mother would have packed for a trip.

She was from Equador, estranged from her husband, and—according to the nun who directed the educational center for immigrant women and their children and had helped these for two years—fleeing a situation that threatened her custody of the four boys, who were "beautiful, quiet, sweet, respectful." She herself, the director said, was "not a crazy woman, as some of her family and friends are making out. She was a darn good mother, a wonderful mother."

Her last act, according to the engineer of the train, was to try to get one son, on the opposite side of the tracks from her and the other three, to their side. They were all in the middle when—after blowing the whistle and applying the brakes—he was unable to avoid hitting them with a train traveling seventy-one miles per hour. Yet some considered her "crazy" for seeking an unknown haven for her family. That word, too, rang hollow in my ears when I remembered having it used about me.

It took a tragedy like this for even two people to defend the woman as a mother: a nun who knew her and her children, a man who was the last to see them alive. But I was with her instinctively, before her identity was disclosed. You don't lead four children along a railroad track to effect a quintuple suicide, even if you know there isn't time to get off before a fast train hits you, which she didn't. When I found out she was the overworked pregnant custodian who stopped her scrubbing to smile at a puppy, I regarded her as that elusive mother superior. Not because she was literally superior but because the scant evidence so conclusively revealed her commitment to a demanding role.

The woman didn't have the leisure to give herself over to motherhood as I did with the puppies. Nearly half her time was devoted to a low-paying, back-breaking job that couldn't provide for her children. Nor could she freely enjoy them when she wasn't at work; people wanted to take them away from her. Obviously she needed them, as I needed my puppies. But real mothers of any economic class are seldom free from other obligations the way I was when Poco died. I can finally see the rearing of her litter as a privilege.

··23··

The brood bitch herself also enjoys this privilege. If she does indeed have a job—like herding her owner's cows in the case of a corgi doing what it was bred for—she gets a full leave to nurse her litter. She owes nothing to the sire, who may not even live on the premises. She is free to nurse, lick, clean her puppies all day, all night, every day. Her devotion and pleasure are enviable.

My most memorable observation of a brood bitch's devotion was also the saddest. She had lost six of her seven puppies on Christmas Eve with an on-call vet. Although he did a Caesarean section for the last three, when she was already exhausted from having been induced with oxytocin for the others, she was in apparent bliss caring for the single survivor. With a fresh incision in her abdomen she curled herself around her baby, cuddling it next to her. She fed it, cleaned it, nuzzled it, always keeping it close to her abdomen, which never seemed to hurt despite a developing infection. Even when the puppy died the next day, she didn't reject it, as bitches usually do, by pushing it into a corner. I had to take it away from her, and I have never seen such a forlorn mother.

Suddenly, however, her ears went up and she was alert, looking out of her box across the room. I followed her gaze to a porcelain corgi statue, about the size of her puppy, given to me the day before and accepted with grief and gratitude. I didn't know then how grateful I would be for this temporary relief of my bitch's sorrow. I picked it up and debated whether to put it in the box with her. Cruel, I decided: it was colder than the dead puppy. I could let her smell it, feel it; she deserved to know. Finally, though, I left it where it was, to allow her the illusion as long as it would last—the rest of that miserable Christmas day.

I had gotten this bitch as an adult, shortly after Paddington died. She was his great-granddaughter and ideal in type and bloodlines for Pesto, who was my only corgi at the time. The litter would have been a family affair. But she got nothing out of it except an infection, a scar, and a total loss of coat, such as all bitches experience after whelping. And a postpartum depression, which I have never seen in a bitch whose litter lived. If the cause is hormonal, as they say about women, why does a brood bitch escape it?

The one who didn't already had the infection during her twenty-four hours of bliss with her puppy, and it was treated aggressively the next day. But even when her temperature went down and she began to eat normally, she languished. Pesto—put out at being almost totally ignored for several days—was eager to resume life as usual. The bitch, however, moped for three or four weeks, the time she would have been nursing her pups.

Seeing her despair over losing a litter probably initiated my unconscious shift to the brood bitch's point of view, though I hadn't known this one since birth. Losing Poco and nursing her puppies myself ten years later completed it. Only in the year following that painful pleasure did I begin to understand how motherhood could have been and, perhaps, could be. You are a mother for life; in the normal course of things your child will outlive you, unlike your bitch, whom you cherish as long as you have her. Why not your daughter, regardless of her ages and stages, which you tolerate in your dogs?

Before Poco my profound losses were two males who had each done all I asked over ten years—been loving, loyal, well-trained companions; gone through the show-ring paces to become champions; bred quality bitches to produce about a dozen litters each. Both had similar old-age problems—urinary and/or prostatic infections, with impaired continence as the presenting symptom. Given how readily corgis are house-trained and how long a healthy one can go without an accident (twelve hours or more), I look back in amazement at the amount of urine I cleaned up from Paddington and Pesto as a part of routine care.

My patience, of course, was due to a decade of increasing love, as well as a sense of impending loss, which I hoped to postpone, though I eventually euthanized each, rather than have him suffer from an incurable illness. Poco appeared to suffer very little, but she almost died in my face, without my consent, let alone my assistance. Why this blow should enlighten me about motherhood, even before I took over for her, was not clear at the time and is still something I see through a glass darkly.

··24··

s with my male corgis, it was years of love and the possibility of loss which precipitated my profoundest commitment to my husband. We were separated, but we continued to talk; I even asked him over for a drink on occasion after Jennifer was in bed. We had things in common besides her, and I missed his company. One evening he told me that he sometimes had such an urge to jump out the window of his fifth-floor apartment he had to make himself read student papers to avoid doing it. I took the revelation lightly, as an instance of Joseph Conrad's "choice of nightmares," one of my husband's favorite phrases. But I did mention it to my psychiatrist. That was the only time he ever actually told me to do anything: "If you feel any responsibility for his life, you should report what he said to his therapist."

I followed orders, though I disliked the woman who ran his therapy group, which included psychotics. She responded coolly, saying she would take what I said under advisement. After their next meeting, I called my husband to see if she had mentioned it. She hadn't, so I did. He should be in a hospital, I told him. He agreed. On my psychiatrist's advice we went to St. Luke's emergency, which admitted him.

I visited him every night during his three-week stay. I have no idea now who took care of our daughter those evenings. Babysitters in New York expected to be escorted to wherever they lived; while there was a reliable teenager on Tenth Street whom I could walk home (leaving Jennifer alone for the time it took), I believe I found her only later. I can recall occasionally walking some woman to a taxi, a few blocks from Weehawken Street and paying the driver her fare, but not as often as I was at St. Luke's.

My total commitment then was to my husband, his life, hence the blank I draw on Jennifer. I'm sure she was in good hands; her father didn't even ask after her, let alone accuse me of neglect. We were involved in an intense romance, beyond the real world. As the weeks passed, however, and we talked about his coming "home," I wasn't sure he should.

It would be unfair to Jennifer to be teased by any uncertainty. I was immensely relieved when he told me his attending psychiatrist had said that if I didn't want him to live with me, he'd better find someplace else because he was going to be discharged. I was grateful to the doctor as well as my husband for telling me what he'd said. I would never be his wife again, but I would always be Jennifer's mother. This may have been the first time I shifted my concern for us, the couple that became a family, to my daughter.

··25··

*I*ronically my single-minded commitment to my doctorate took place in the psychiatric ward of the same hospital, where I spent twelve hours a day, seven days a week, for three weeks, typing my dissertation. Although my two-hour orals had been the scariest part, it was at the last stage that I panicked. I realized I had no idea how long it would take me to type the final draft. The magic three weeks—to have a nurse for Jennifer, to rescue a suicidal husband, to nurture a litter of puppies—was in my head as adequate for the job, perhaps because that was the minimum required by professional typists.

I must have believed in magic to think I could type at the rate of the professionals. But my project, an edition of medieval lyrics about women in a thirteenth-century manuscript, required Middle English characters not on a traditional typewriter. So I bought an Olympia fitted out with them for $150, less than the typists charged to do a standard dissertation. Mine was much more complicated and would have been an expensive job, liable to errors by the best of typists.

I had met my own deadline for a draft that incorporated the suggestions of my two advisers. During that time I was also firing off letters to some forty colleges and universities close enough to New

York for Jennifer to see her father at least once a month, preferably more often. They all promised to keep my application on file.

As the time dwindled to three weeks before Columbia's dead-line—March 15, when most job openings were filled—I despaired on two counts: I wouldn't be able to meet it, and I wouldn't get a job if I did. I couldn't raise Jennifer on a part-time salary and her father's child support, nor could I type a dissertation and take care of her.

My resentment focused on Jennifer; because of her I didn't have a choice of jobs all over the country, nor could I finish my degree and hack it as an adjunct until I found what I wanted. At age six she could not be expected to know or care what getting a Ph.D. meant to me, with all the worst behind me. Neither could I risk throwing it over on her account.

My psychiatrist helped solve the problem. We discussed the options of getting someone to take care of Jennifer. Her father could have done that in his loft, but her response to our separation included a fear of staying with him. A twelve-hour-a-day sitter was out of the question financially. I knew my mother would come from South Carolina, but I couldn't expect her to run the house and look after Jennifer as if I were not there. That was it, I realized: I couldn't be there.

I don't remember which of us suggested a hospital. Quite pos-sibly I did, and if not, I was definitely amenable. He thought he could get me into Mt. Sinai (which I perceived as the source of my present quandary because Jennifer was born there) or St. Luke's (which had saved my husband and given us a last romantic idyll). What determined our choice was that only St. Luke's would allow me to bring a typewriter and have a private room.

In the days preceding the reprieve that I felt sure would save my doctorate, I arranged every detail of my mother's trip and stay, delegated the tasks with which she'd need help to my husband, left precise instructions and maps for getting where she had to go, and wrote volumes of information about Jennifer's care. I don't yet know how I persuaded a young daughter and a provincial mother that I wasn't crazy, even though I was entering a psychiatric ward, but I invited them to visit me after I got settled.

They came once. While I had hardly noticed the other patients when I visited my husband, I did now. So did Jennifer and my mother. They met me in the hospital, and I took them out for tea, since I had no restrictions about leaving the ward. This awkward visit was early in my stay, something I wanted to get done as soon as possible. My phone contact with them was minimal because there was only one telephone for the patients, all of whom wanted to be on it. Except me.

Instead I established my rigorous schedule. By eight A.M. I had showered, eaten breakfast, and begun to type. I spent less than an hour a day at meals; not only was the food unappetizing but the atmosphere was disturbing. The only time I enjoyed eating was the nine P.M. snack, which consisted of sandwiches freshly made on our floor. At that point I was finished typing for the day and looked forward to the food and even the company—of one person.

He was a Yale M.D. in residence at a New York hospital, a paranoid schizophrenic from whom I learned a lot about commitment to a profession. He had gotten far enough in his career to become a resident but would "have to learn to live with mental illness," he said. Already he had blown it, having been hospitalized after locking himself in his room and refusing to answer either medical or personal calls. I would finish my dissertation and eventually get a job, which I would keep. He would be in and out of mental hospitals.

He was smart and witty; we went out a couple of evenings, with me as his "buddy," to a Columbia dive. Over beer, which I think was forbidden, his talk of breeding a superior race alarmed me. Like my husband, whose first name he had, he was Jewish. This Nazi philosophy was strange to hear from him. But then he was "crazy," not like the mother with her children on the railroad tracks, not like me with Jennifer out in the rain, not like the doctoral candidate finishing a dissertation in the hospital, not even like my estranged husband with suicidal impulses. He had an incurable psychosis.

This recognition of F. Scott Fitzgerald's greatest of all differences between men — that between the sick and the well — stayed with me a long time after I saw my doctoral adviser to tell him I had completed my dissertation. "Oh," he said, "I was so worried when they told me you were in the hospital. I thought you were really sick." What it was and where I was didn't strike him as unusual; I was among the living and functioning. I would later see the difference in dogs: Poco when her breathing changed, her puppy limp among wriggling littermates.

··26··

Seeing this vast difference between the sick and the well, you commit to wellness: keep your daughter's fever in check, get your depressed husband into a hospital, prevent yourself from abandoning ten years of work. You don't die with your children like the woman on the tracks, your husband doesn't become a lifelong mental patient like his namesake, you don't forfeit your career. Your bitch dies and you save her puppies; the prettiest one dies and you keep the others alive.

But what you really commit to is life itself—the deepest implication of motherhood. Wellness is a park-mother concern. A brood bitch will nose a sick puppy into a corner and ignore it until it dies. Poco would have done that with the puppy I held until she gasped her last breath. Until I raised her orphans, I was a park mother despite my contempt for the type. It took the untimely death of my brood bitch to teach me what motherhood was really about: puppies must *live,* via twenty-four-hour-a-day nurture for three weeks—no nurse. Nurses are for privileged human mothers.

Fitzgerald's observation about the sick and the well implies the difference between the privileged and the nonprivileged, the living and the dead. In *The Great Gatsby* the privileged end up alive, most notoriously the faux mother, Daisy Buchanan, whose "blessed precious" daughter was—at three—still under the exclusive care of a nurse. The others die, including the bitch puppy Tom Buchanan bought from a street vendor for his mistress Myrtle; it was the closest thing she would have to a child with him or her husband. After she was killed by Daisy, the only reference to the puppy is Tom's professed grief on finding its collar and leash among Myrtle's effects.

If my human commitments were privileged for all concerned, so too, was the one to Poco's puppies. Not only did I have full time to give them, but I also had the means to ensure their safe delivery by a superior vet. Their very existence was the result of two decades of studying corgis—breeding the best to the best and hoping for the best. My commitment to raising them properly almost guaranteed good lives for them, unlike Fitzgerald's hopelessly misbegotten puppies being hawked outside Grand Central Station like half-dead flowers for a man to buy for his lonely mistress.

In reality the privileged are also subject to death's dominion. It claimed Poco even as she was giving life. All my yesteryears of book-mothering, gut-mothering, even park-mothering my daughter were wiped out when my brood bitch died. Then I was forced to be a good mother. It wasn't a skill I finally learned, an instinct that at last kicked in. It was an imperative with rewards I had never known.

··27··

here was something else about Poco's death besides raising her puppies that enlightened me about Jennifer. She too had been with me since a difficult delivery—upside down, backwards, and out of the sac. She ended up as my pick of the litter, a bitch to "have some fun with," as we say of a nice puppy we will enjoy showing. But the fun was cut short by her untimely death. That was not the reason I hadn't had much fun with my daughter.

I myself had cut off the opportunities after several apparent impasses. I don't mean her being almost wholly incommunicable, as she was the summer before she left for college. While I could appreciate her anxiety, even about leaving a mother she didn't appear to like, I thought she had everything to look forward to. She had been accepted on early application to Mount Holyoke. This was my idea, one of two decisions toward which I actually pushed her as a teenager. I wanted to avoid rejections because of her mediocre SATs and possibly secure her admission to a college I believed would look favorably on committed applicants, one where she could find those sisters she never had. It was her absolute top choice, she said.

Yet on the day of her departure storms erupted between us as well as outside, where a hurricane broke several large limbs, one of which hung perilously over the walk we would use to load the van her father had rented to take her to South Hadley. As I leaned from a tiny attic window trying to dislodge it, she whined about my inattention to this important day in her life. She wasn't a child crying because the house burned down and she couldn't have her birthday party; she was an eighteen-year-old annoyed that a storm had interfered with her departure from a home she seemed to hate. I sent her packing: "You're an adult now. This is no longer where you live. Don't use the address."

This was cruel of me, a last blast at a daughter I could never make happy. She didn't use the address, even to write. But a month later, for her birthday, I splurged on a hand-woven, brilliantly colored afghan to cheer up her room and warm her when it got cold. She thanked me. We were polite but distant and we never lived together again.

I did learn a bit more about her after she left, from several black-and-white speckled notebooks she left on the top of a box labeled "DO NOT THROW." I picked up one of them, expecting to see her high-school class notes. Instead I found a letter-diary to a nonexistent female friend. I read a few pages and debated whether to go on; I did, but with the vow not to torture myself. In her place I would have taken them with me or "thrown" them.

Some entries were not surprising in the relationship they described between us, from "I really love my mother" to "I hate her." The former was illustrated with an example I barely recalled: "She bought me a wine-colored leather handbag and said to think of it as an investment." The latter, curiously, had to do with the dogs: "She didn't even give them breakfast until noon." Since I feed my dogs twice a day, I never felt obliged to keep a strict time schedule, and the hostility—as well as the concern—in this entry surprised me.

The bulk of the entries concentrated in great detail on boys she liked who seemed to have little interest in her, including one about whom she repeatedly complained to me because he harassed her on the school bus—took her mittens, threw her hat out the window. I even called the school and reported him, the selfsame object of her account of some thrilling attention he paid her. I could understand her reluctance to discuss any of this with me, and the notebooks explained all the time she spent isolated in her room.

But she was gone now, and holidays—which had always been difficult—became more so. In her only-child-of-divorced-parents mode she acted as if she were doing her father or me a favor by letting us take turns having her on Thanksgiving or Christmas. It wasn't that she wanted us all together either.

Twice he and I planned Christmas dinner *en famille*. Once we had it in Southport, and even with the dull boyfriend we also invited, Jennifer was surly. The other was to be at a New York restaurant, but she begged for a ticket to Boulder to share it with some of her father's relatives and he gave in. So I went to New York to have dinner alone with him.

It was bitterly cold. After a bottle of champagne at his loft, he suggested we scrap the restaurant and get deli takeout. I heartily agreed. Steaming chicken soup and hot pastrami sandwiches, with more champagne, comprised the best Christmas dinner I'd had since Jennifer was born. There was—besides the food and drink—a warm understanding between my ex-husband and me about her. We didn't talk about it, we just felt what had drawn us together besides the mutual desire for a baby girl. Nobody had sent her packing that day. She chose an expensive trip away from us as a Christmas present.

This wasn't cruel on her part, just insensitive. Her cruelty came years later, when my mother died. She had been a good grandmother to Jennifer: besides staying with her when I was in the hospital, she had also come up later when I was more happily engaged giving lectures on a cruise ship. And she regularly sent gifts, cards, and letters that revealed her understanding of this particular grandchild. I expected Jennifer to be upset when I called with the news of her death. She was, I think, but she was vague about going to the funeral. After routine questions about when and where she would be flying from, I finally asked her point blank if she planned to go. No. Why? She didn't want to say. I pressed. She didn't like being with me when I was upset.

I swallowed that. She was right to the extent that most of our visits home usually included a standoff between me and my mother. But she was dead now. When my father died—four months before her—my terminally ill mother said "No parade," and we respected her wishes for a simple funeral. Hers was something else: even I agreed it should be in the church. Between Sunday school and sixth grade she had taught practically everybody in town. People of all ages would want to come. And they did. Ironically the church service was the only time I wasn't lonely; my sister and I walked down the aisle together and sat by ourselves in the first pew. After that—at the graveside and the house—Jennifer's absence was conspicuous to others and painful to me.

Immediately afterwards I left for a literary seminar in Key West. Both the airline and the guesthouse had been sympathetic to my several changes of plan while my mother was dying. When a flight attendant in Charlotte asked how things had gone at the funeral, I started to cry—but about Jennifer, not my mother. Her I would mourn late at night as I read my "Baby Book" in my secluded room.

I never kept such a book for Jennifer when she was a baby because I considered them silly. And while I was reading my own, I didn't think she deserved one. Now I don't know. Mine was written in the third person to me: "Mother loves you so much. Her mother died when she was six. She loves her stepmother, but it isn't the same as her real mother. You are named after her. Mother wants to live a long time for you." There was a lot to think about in that entry.

She did love me, she did live a long time, but there was never much rapport between us. Despite the fact that she had a college education, with a degree in music, and a teaching career she resumed when my sister and I got out of grade school, we were very different. She couldn't have predicted this; no mother can of a child. But did she even recognize it? Or did she always think I was wrong, as I felt most of the time? I'm sure she didn't, any more than I thought Jennifer was. Maybe, like me with my daughter, she considered herself wrong.

Jennifer must also have felt the difference between her mother and stepmother. Was that why she made fun of her? At times I told her she was an ingrate, but at others I joined in the fun-making: because she was so unbelievably sweet, we called her such things as "the fairy stepmother" or "Swiss chocolate." She was much more like my mother than I was. Yet Jennifer and I were about as different as personalities can be, according to Myers-Briggs personality assessment tests. I scoffed at the time, but I've since wondered what you should do in such a case. You probably wouldn't choose the person as a spouse or roommate, but you don't have a choice with children.

I also wonder if Myers-Briggs picks up a sense of humor in character-typing. That is what my mother and Jennifer's stepmother lacked. My father had a good one, and while he was neglectful as a parent, I got along much better with him when I was an adult than I did with my mother. He could make and take a joke. This possibility exists for me and Jennifer because she has a sense of humor that I see when we find the same things funny—especially in literature. But it was hard to perceive when we were making each other unhappy. And while it may be anthropomorphizing, anyone who knows corgis claims their sense of humor as a breed trait.

··28··

*P*oco wasn't an amusing corgi, however, and that may have been why I wasn't able to "have fun with her" during the four years of her life. I liked her primarily as a beautiful specimen of the breed. At seven months she was Best Puppy at our regional corgi club's annual match, but after that I showed her only once. I didn't really enjoy all-breed shows any more, though they were what got me into breeding corgis. I preferred specialty shows, where you hoped for a placement or compliments from other breeders. Or just admiring my own at home.

But at home with Poco I mostly yelled at her to stop barking, which she did at everything—four-legged, two-legged, four-wheeled, two-wheeled—that passed the house. One of the few pictures I have of her, taken from outside the stairway window where she liked to sit, shows her lovely head and neck spoiled by something shiny above her. It was, I remembered, a Slinky toy I had hung there in an effort to scare her away from her favorite barking perch.

I chose another photo—as a blooming adolescent in a pen on the porch—for her obituary, with a quote from Wordsworth: "She seemed a thing that could not feel / The touch of earthly years." This was true, but it also meant she would never grow up, like her mother, Tempo, who had a similarly excitable temperament and whom I had carefully placed in a one-dog home with a mature couple who wanted a lively corgi "to keep us young and laughing."

It was a perfect match, of the sort nature doesn't make between mothers and daughters or even between breeders and picks of the litter, a choice you don't overtly make with children. Moreover Tempo's new owners, with whom I became friends, were quite fond of Poco. We had a half-spoken understanding that she was next in line for the throne at their house. In other words, in words for the first time, I didn't plan to keep Poco all of her life. Only the accident of her early death kept her with me for the whole of it. Neither my grief nor my single-minded attention to her puppies obscured this sad fact, on which I was inclined to brood.

It wasn't the idea of placing Poco that made me feel bad. Most corgi fanciers who breed on a small scale like me—a litter every couple of years—and keep only two or three adults find good homes for an occasional retired stud dog or brood bitch. Too many corgis at large in the house, even if it's Buckingham Palace, can trigger fights and bloodshed. You need crates and gates and an ever-watchful eye with as few as four of them.

But some you keep as long as they live because they're special. This was true of Paddington and Pesto, both of whom I had castrated years before they died to relieve prostatic hypertrophy. It wasn't just that they were males—which I admittedly preferred—as I had placed a handsome Paddington son, Bedford. He challenged his sire over everything from bitches to food to dogs outside the fence. More than once I incurred deep puncture wounds breaking up fights, and in the last one he serrated his father's ear. He spent his final weeks at home in a crate, until he went off in that crate on the leather back seat of a Mercedes-Benz with a couple who adored him.

You have—and play—favorites with dogs, an unacceptable option with children. Having only Jennifer, I didn't encounter this problem, but as the firstborn myself, I felt my sister was favored, at least by our father. Our mother said she always "tried" to treat us equally. This led me to believe it was an effort on her part. I was astonished when my sister told me in middle age that she thought *I* was the "pet." That word tells a lot, about people and dogs, and its etymology for animals is obscure. I am proud that my corgis are house pets—no kennels, no runs, no basement, just individual crates for each of them to use at will as adults or be confined to as puppies in my absence. The pets of my pets, however, were the two male corgis who lived out their lives with me.

Was Poco born so bad that I wouldn't want her for life? Or was it that I sequestered her from her mother, who wasn't pleased to have this puppy stay with us? Should I have let Tempo discipline her? It is commonly believed that an adult wouldn't really hurt a puppy, who wouldn't be likely to fight back, but I didn't like those bared maternal teeth. And I knew differently about mothers and daughters. In any case Tempo went to her new, only-dog home when Poco was five months old, and I was able to let her join the household with me and Pesto, her grandfather.

My effort to get a three-generation photograph just before Tempo left was disastrous, except for showing the refined family type, a light red with a white muzzle and blaze, pale masking on the cheeks, very dark eyes and eye rims. Pesto looked bored, Tempo annoyed, and Poco frantic to get out of the pen. What my pictures often reveal, on later inspection, is a definite temperamental trait. This one reminded me of the Slinky to discourage Poco's barking and indicated that she was certainly hyperactive, even if she hadn't yet started to bark excessively.

All dogs bark, and with people at the door or late night noises, you usually want them to. The UPS, FedEx, garbage, and mailmen are standard "acceptable" causes, though you wish they weren't. Other dogs may also be a cause, but you could do without it, especially if there are a lot of them. Pesto considered all of the above to be barkable, and Poco's eventual excess seemed competitive: to call somebody's attention to herself, she had to bark more. None of my dogs, her included, ever engaged in what I call "mindless barking," where they just stand in the yard, house, car, or even a vet's office and bark nonstop. These nobody can stand. I probably minded Poco's barking more than any of the objects of it.

Despite her competitiveness about barking and everything else around the house and yard, she didn't compete in the show ring, perhaps sensing my aversion to it. I took her to one all-breed show when she was just a year old, under a judge I knew would like her type. Corgis were scheduled at eight A.M. on Easter morning in Providence, and we left at five to allow time for her to get used to the site, which appeared to be a hockey rink. The more she saw the less she became used to it. There was a great deal of equipment being banged around, a lot of large dogs raced along the sidelines by professional handlers, much crackling over loudspeakers, and the inevitable scratchy recording of the national anthem.

"What on earth is wrong with her?" the judge asked me, cautioning me to hold her tightly to keep her from jumping off the examining table. "First dog show," I muttered in gloomy response. She tried hard to get a good look at Poco, who I think ended up fifth in a class of six. She asked me as we left the ring how old she was, then said reassuringly: "Nice bitch. Work on her." What this judge didn't know was how much I worked to *contain* her at home. Show-training on top of that was too much. Hence my never "having fun with her" in the ring, which I no longer considered much fun anyhow.

After Pesto died, when Poco was three, I hoped to bond with her. She was all I had, and I thought that being the only dog would make her more responsive to me. But in the year before I bred her there was little change in her behavior. I did love our month together in Maine, in a remote cottage on the water with no distractions; the peace made me seriously consider giving up the Southport house I had rented for twenty-seven years in favor of something in the country. Now that I have Psallenda, who doesn't even bark at the mailman and loves the attention of passersby, whom she attracts by quietly running alongside the fence, I am amazed that a fractious bitch could have led me to consider such a drastic move.

..29..

I did think Poco's possessiveness might make her a good mother. Breeders sometimes say a bitch "needs a litter," to mature her body and/or give her confidence and calm her down. But her mother was no calmer after three litters. Whether Poco was an example of the fruit not falling far from the tree or the environment her mother and I provided for her, I will never know. I do know that—without any canine role model—Psallenda isn't a barker. And it's generally believed that hand-raised puppies bond closely with their eventual human caregivers. This is certainly true of Psallenda and her littermates. The question I want to avoid keeps insinuating itself into my consciousness: was it best for all concerned that Poco died?

I dislike the answer more than the question and can appreciate it only conditionally. If Poco had lived and rejected the puppies because of the C-section, and if an ideal owner had wanted a beautiful house-trained adult bitch, I might have let her go when she was fully recovered from the surgery. I had already decided, after the uterine inertia, not to breed her again. But it would have been hard to dump a new mother after a traumatic delivery. Although I might later have been able to say we were all better off, including

Poco in a new home, I would still feel bad about "getting rid of her" because she failed at a job I didn't do well either.

But she died, giving me her chance—and mine—to be a good mother. I would never have bought this with Poco's life. Yet having hand-raised her mother's second litter, which was an elective C-section immediately followed by a gastrotomy to remove pieces of plastic she had ingested during pregnancy, when she couldn't be under anesthesia, I already knew that it was easier without having to care for a post-op bitch hostile to her puppies.

I had tried to coax this bitch, Tempo, into nursing the litter when her milk finally came down, delayed by two surgeries, but I had to hold her while they suckled and she trembled—whether from pain or anxiety I wasn't sure. I was aware she had bitten one when the vet put it on her at the hospital, so I decided to take no chances. Instead I dried her up by withholding all food for a day and gradually increasing it to the normal amount. And kept her away from the puppies. And combed out the postpartum effluvium, as they call the shed. Yes, if I had to hand-raise puppies, there was an advantage in not having to worry about the brood bitch.

That is as close as I can bring myself to answering the question raised by Poco's death. If she had lived and matured after raising her litter, I might have learned something of what I now know about motherhood. She might have showed me what I missed thirty-five years ago when I remained essentially unchanged after Jennifer's birth.

Possibly I was ready for that change—whether Poco lived or died. Her death enabled me to think about coming to terms with her: not "having fun" in the ring, not yelling when she barked, not even imagining what pretty puppies she could make. Just enjoying an adult friendship. This is a fantasy that an untimely death allows us, and it may be no more than that.

The opportunity I lost with Poco still exists with Jennifer. Having become a good mother to orphan puppies, I finally understood a line from a medieval poem I used to quote to her when I was studying for my orals: "Patience is a point, though it displease oft." I didn't get it for thirty years. With luck—and patience—my daughter might get it sooner.

··*30*··

*I*f I myself am patient, I can believe that the worst of Jennifer's and my relationship is behind us. I didn't write her off when she refused to go to my mother's funeral. I simply tried to maintain a noninvasive relationship: birthday and holiday gifts, but no invitations and few conversations. In one of these—and I have repressed the occasion—she prefaced some remark with "Since I stopped speaking to you a year an a half ago. . . ." We must have been talking about motherhood, because I told her she came from a line of bad mothers and might not want to have children.

This was true: my mother had lost hers when she was six and didn't feel the same about her stepmother. She loved me and my sister but didn't seem comfortable with us, as children or adults. We were both professionally successful—earned doctorates and got university jobs—but we each divorced and had trouble with our daughters.

Jennifer's response to my comment stunned me: "If I never have a child it will be because I don't want to be a mother like you." I let that pass at the time and tried to remember when it was she had stopped speaking to me. Going back a year and a half, I realized it was when my mother died. Since I was quite down then, unable to be aggressive toward her or anyone else, I was truly puzzled. Ultimately I decided to respond—with a letter of which I kept a copy, though I later destroyed it.

There were other reasons she might not have a child, I wrote. She might not find anyone who wanted to have one with her. Or she might not be able to conceive. Or she might decide she didn't want the responsibility. Or she might not want one who turned out like her. I added something else I had deliberately never said to her: how much more privileged her own childhood had been than mine. This was our darkest moment. At the time I thought it might be our last communication, and I didn't even care. But then her father died.

His death was as shocking as Poco's in that I almost witnessed it. I called to tell him that a new biography of Edith Wharton, which he was eager to read, had finally come out. A strange male voice answered and asked if I wanted to speak to his wife. Yes, please. "Oh God, I think he's gone." Then to the paramedic who had picked up the phone: "No, don't put the blanket over his head."

Within minutes I had called his son, who confirmed that my ex-husband was dead, and our daughter, who already knew from her half-brother. We cried together, there being nothing to say. But I felt we were close.

Months later, however, at the memorial service for him in New York City, of which I had received the same formal notice as everyone else, I found Jennifer inaccessible. Not, it appeared, from grief, as she gave a warm and witty tribute to him. She pulled away when I hugged her and told her how sorry I was.

··*31*··

*C*learly death, as a shared sorrow, would never bring me and my daughter closer. Only reflections on a private loss related to motherhood, I realized a few years later, could possibly bring about mutual forgiveness. That loss was the death of Poco. Jennifer is, after all, still alive to "have some fun with."

She gave signs of wanting a *rapprochement* when she became engaged. Ironically the occasion was Mother's Day; she and her fiancé wanted to take me to brunch. His parents and stepmother were all dead so I speculated that he might be urging a reconciliation with the one remaining parent between them. Or possibly she wanted to show me off to him: he was working as an adult on a degree in English. Could she finally be proud to introduce me as her mother?

As things turned out, it seemed she was simply emboldened by having him as a buffer in the meeting with me. She told me over brunch that she had lost her job, and he held her hand tightly as if to protect her. I said the usual supportive things to her, after which he and I engaged in a fairly formal discussion of literature.

Later she seemed as uncomfortable as ever in the house I had told her fifteen years earlier was no longer her home. She took her fiancé up to see her room and appeared upset that I had altered it for my own use. Neither was interested in the dogs, Pesto and Poco, though she had known Pesto; he said the breed he might want was a bichon frisé, that he had some friends who showed Dobermans. I couldn't work up much enthusiasm for this dog conversation.

But the meeting was a start, I told myself, and six months later I invited them for Thanksgiving dinner at a local restaurant. When Jennifer accepts my invitations she always informs me how early she has to be home, so I avoided that downer by suggesting three P.M. They arrived a bit early but refused all offers of a drink, from champagne to beer to sparkling cider to diet Coke. During dinner and desultory conversation, my eyes and thoughts wandered to a man eating alone and appearing to enjoy it. I envied him the lack of family baggage, the boldness to have a nice dinner by himself.

My guests, my daughter and her husband-to-be, were on the road less than two hours after their arrival. I was back with my dogs and the sparkling cider. And more reflections. We'd had a good meal, but not much communication. She was inaccessible, as I had learned many times over in trying to talk to her or get her to talk.

Perhaps this is the supreme advantage in relating to dogs. You hear about their absolute devotion to you, no matter what you do, but I'm not so sure of that, at least as it applies to corgis. They do take offense: board them, for example, come back expecting the warm welcome you always receive at home, and they may act indifferently to you. They get over it, of course; they are definitely more forgiving than children. But the best part is that you don't have to have a discussion with them about whatever is at issue.

Some corgis do "talk" to you. Psallenda does it with a sort of yodel when I wake up in the morning. Since she's been on the bed all night, it's clearly an acknowledgment of my conscious existence on a new day. Pesto, on the other hand, didn't volunteer any morning greeting. If I hugged him on first awakening, he might emit a soft growl, no lifted lips or anything, just not a high-spirited "Good day." His morning talk was more like mine—grumpy—but I find

Psallenda's cheerful variety appealing, as I never found any human being's. I even respond to it on occasion.

These, to be sure, do not amount to conversations, let alone discussions, nor does my addressing the dogs in ordinary English, which I usually do. Their being "dumb" or nonverbal animals is possibly their greatest gift to their adoptive best friend. Not only do they spare us all the awkward, unpleasant, fruitless discussions with human intimates, they also relieve us of the hostile silences.

Psallenda once vividly illustrated the dog's way of communicating. Having found a flea on her, I bathed her, sprayed the house, and decided to get rid of her basket of toys I couldn't spray—mostly fleece animals that variously quacked, mooed, or crowed when she took them in her mouth. Furtively I removed them first to a paper bag and onto the porch, then into a plastic garbage bag. She watched with justified suspicion as I took it toward the can. The duck made one last quack-quack-quack-quack; she knew and she was angry. I gave her some older toys stored in a different place to tide her over until the arrival of an extravagant supply of new ones I ordered. But she spurned them.

Two days later I showed her the new duck, rooster, goat, cow, pig, monkey, and violin. The last *I* found appealing, especially when I discovered it played the Bach "Anna Magdalene Notebook." She didn't toss them about and activate the sounds as usual. Instead she took all but the violin to the back of her crate, then curled up in front, facing me. She didn't resist my taking them away, but she successfully conveyed her distrust.

Her rejection of the violin was her most subtle message: you got it for yourself, you like the Bach, *you* play with it. But her forgiveness was obvious when she shortly took to the replacement animals. A few days later it was downright sublime when she chose the violin first and played the whole piece. This was a nonverbal concession of the sort Jennifer seldom offered.

··*32*··

*I*n contrast with the corgis, Jennifer's and my inability to communicate, in words or silence, represents a deeper dysfunction. Not only is there the line of bad mothers I mentioned to her but also the probability that every member of our little nuclear family—her father, her mother, and she—suffered some form of personality disorder.

His psychiatrist put it to him early on: he couldn't relate to people, with the emphasis on people. I took that lightly, assuming it meant he was fine with his cats and his work. I knew he was professionally and socially accomplished. That I didn't heed this warning about intimate relationships and married him anyway was a clue to *my* disorder. I too was at ease in professional and social relationships, though I hadn't yet found corgis. But I couldn't be happily married to him or anyone else, a predictable outcome of my previous string of lovers and my eventual professional independence, fortified by my commitment to corgis.

The progeny of such parents, as we would say in breeding two dogs with questionable temperaments, could be expected to have problems. Maybe Jennifer's crying was the first manifestation, not helped by nurture from parents like us. In the dog, at least, you have a chance of also eliminating the environmental contributions: the sire usually makes none and in Psallenda's case, neither did the dam. In Jennifer's, however, both of us did. Her difficulty in making friends, keeping a job, or finding a husband should have been no surprise. Or her devotion to cats. She needed something to relate to, and her father's choice of pet, which he resumed after our divorce, may have seemed less exclusive than mine, though her working hours were always better suited to cats than dogs.

She has, at least, caught up with her parents professionally, being the librarian for a city newspaper. Before that, she worked for a while at McDonald's, was fired from a job in a food service, quit another with an insurance company where she wasn't getting anywhere, and lost a directorship of admissions in a small law school, one she liked. It apparently figured in her and her fiancé's long-range plans, as he intended to go on for a degree in law. That they married anyway, without the free tuition for him, suggests a better ability to "relate to people" than either parent.

The wedding, however, was a low point for me. I dislike them generally, the bigger the worse, and hers was fairly big, on the second anniversary of her father's death. It was the first day of summer, two weeks into the six I booked at the Maine cottage to celebrate my retirement. Their original date was in May, but they changed it to accommodate the minister's schedule. I dealt with the inconvenience by settling for four weeks in Maine and accepting the unfortunate confluence of three significant family events: her marriage, his death, my retirement.

It was held in Massachusetts, saving me about a hundred miles on an indirect trip to Maine that would total over four hundred. The obvious choice was to go the night before, but none of the motels nearby accepted dogs. Jennifer owned a two-bedroom house, but was putting up her maid of honor and didn't offer me any hospitality. All I really wanted, in the end, was a cool place on her property where I could leave Poco in a crate during the ceremony and reception. But what she suggested was a nearby kennel.

I was so hurt, frustrated, and angry that I went to bed the night before her wedding, my car packed for a month in Maine—my mother-of-the-bride dress in a garment bag—not knowing what I would do in the morning.

I couldn't call the kennel until eight A.M., and in any case I didn't want to dump a dog who could see I had uprooted us from home in a strange place. My alternate plan of leaving her in the car with the hatch open was eliminated by the weather; temperatures were in the nineties throughout Connecticut and Massachusetts. By this time I had ruled out returning home from the wedding and going to Maine the next day—some six hundred miles of driving on consecutive days in extreme heat.

Moreover, after postponing it for two weeks, I badly needed that Maine fix. From the time I had discovered and embraced it— a coast I had resisted because it was so different from the South Carolina beaches I loved as a child—I considered it an ideal retreat for me and my corgis. There was a waterfront peace, not only on the deck where we all spent many hours of long days, but also on the private grounds, where the dogs could run freely. The mid-coast cottage was not so much a vacation spot as a setting in which I could read and write with nothing more distracting than water, islands, and boats.

But since I was now free to do that all year at home, the interruption of my daughter's' wedding ought not to bother me, I decided during the night. After about three hours of sleep I got up, finished packing, called the kennel, gave Poco half a Valium, and set off. That was the trick, I told several people to whom I had complained about the situation. Stop fretting over my daughter's rudeness, tranquilize the *dog*, and everything would be all right. Indeed it was—enjoyable in fact.

The church ceremony, with me in the front pew, brought back the honor I felt at my mother's funeral. Jennifer's tribute to her and to her father in the program completed a sense of peace. The reception-brunch, for which I was truly starved—had I eaten before I left home?—was elegant, and I enjoyed the group of amiable, sophisticated people she had assembled. Still, I was grateful for a reason to leave fairly early: the kennel, her idea, closed at three.

Poco had slept well, without anxiety, and we were on our way. She seemed hardly aware of any interruption in the trip. If I had been able to see past Jennifer's inhospitable behavior, I might have slept better myself. And—now that Poco is asleep forever—I believe I can. I've said more than once that I prefer funerals to weddings because they make people gentler and more forgiving, but I didn't have in mind a dog's last rites.

··*33*··

I hoped marriage would have a forgiving effect on Jennifer. Because she had blown all her money on the wedding, there wasn't anything left for a honeymoon. She said they'd probably just go to a motel for the night. I felt bad for her, as well as pleased that I had stumbled on the perfect gift: a week in Maine, which I knew they both liked. I sent them brochures for three old-fashioned oceanfront inns, of the sort she enjoyed in Block Island, to choose from; they were in the general vicinity of my cottage, but I assured her they would never run into me. They were delighted, and to my surprise invited me to dinner one night.

For once we had a relaxed evening together. And meaningful conversation. We talked about her stepmother, who had moved to a condo in Cologne as soon as her father's estate was settled. She wasn't speaking to her or any of his relatives. We were somewhat mystified by all this, and Jennifer's husband said he couldn't understand why her father had married her in the first place. With a candor that seemed quite natural, I revealed that he told me it was because of her attitude toward and feeling for Jennifer. It was an epiphany for us all as we considered the ramifications: her father loved her that much, the ideal stepmother he chose had tried her best, then deserted her stepdaughter. There must have been unspoken thoughts about me, the natural mother, or so I fancied as we turned our conversation to their future.

Her husband was a year away from his B.A. in English, which he sensibly planned to combine with his knowledge of computer science to get a "real" job. She still worked as the newspaper librarian and had completed half her M.L.S.—commuting across the state to Boston two nights a week.

Jennifer's love of libraries went back to the other decision, besides her application for early admission to college, toward which I pushed her. She was fifteen and planned on returning to camp. Although I knew she didn't want to spend the summer with me, I sensed she was ready for a change, and I suggested she become a page at our local library, which would offer her some money of her own. She went for it and finally found books, though they had surrounded her since birth.

She kept the job two afternoons a week during the school year until she left for college. While we weren't getting along much better, she had a more hospitable environment there than at home, school, or a supermarket cash register. She also had in the avuncular library director a mentor who dared to criticize her choice of reading material, Judy Blume. I never said a word, before then or for a long time afterwards.

But now we were discussing the rainy-day books we had brought to Maine. That was the thing I might miss about teaching, I told them: reading something I really liked and getting thirty students to read and talk about it. I never imagined I could do this with Jennifer, but she had read two of my most successful additions to a course in modern women writers: Anne Tyler's *Ladder of Years* and Harriet Doerr's *Consider This, Señora*. Like Psallenda with the violin, she acknowledged a respect for my taste.

··*34*··

*T*he start of Jennifer's married life marked the beginning
of a new relationship between us. I quickly forgot about
her inconsiderate wedding arrangements, and—more
slowly—my sense of maternal ineptitude.

We all have ways of dealing with this insecurity about mothering. My Oxford cousin eventually left her husband and two children
to study art. When she visited me she said she was on good terms
with all of them and saw them often. She spoke with pride of her
son's maturity and her daughter's beauty. A few years later she
started a successful earthenware ceramic business called "Droll
Designs," which were picked up by the carriage trade.

And—to my surprise—she got a corgi. Her introduction to the
breed occurred one weekend when she was here, and I needed her
to help break up a dog fight. She did as she was told, still in her
nightgown, and grabbed the offending dog, Bedford, while I
picked up poor Paddington, who was bleeding profusely from a
bite in the tongue. I had a puncture wound in the wrist, which I
held in a bucket of warm water for the rest of the day, watching the
gums of a shocky Paddington beside me. My cousin managed to
keep Bedford and the in-season bitch who had provoked the alter-
cation away from us and each other.

The corgi she got despite all this, Clyde, had a "morose" temperament, she told me, not droll like her designs and the typical corgi demeanor. But she sent elaborate Halloween collages, showing Clyde in the sky on angel wings. And for her daughter's wedding the invitations were personalized pieces of her ceramic ware. She got it all together—her daughter, her dog—with her art, which had required years of belated commitment.

My sister didn't yet have her doctorate, her job, or her cats when her daughter moved out. She did, however, have her son—her "spare"—and a Dalmatian. She wasn't obliged to deal with a teenage daughter when she finished her degree and accepted a job halfway across the country. She seemed to enjoy the professional respect, her easy-going son, and the cats she got after she had her dog put down. She was doing fine in her new life—until her daughter's wedding.

This was an elaborate affair in the Midwest where she and the groom grew up and went to college. My sister agonized over every detail that seemed to exclude her: not being put up in the bridal party's section of the motel, not traveling in the limo with her ex-husband and his wife, not having a say about anything. "So don't go," I told her when she complained.

"But she invited me," was her response. Though I pointed out that she probably felt she had to ask her mother, my sister was very much into her mother-of-the-bride role. That she'd already bought her dress was another reason she gave for attending the ceremony. No sense suggesting she take it back, but I did. She finally admitted that she wanted to go—and went.

Some things were worse than she expected, like her daughter's it's-*my*-day attitude, which kept her always at a remove from her mother. But the groom's mother was sympathetic and hospitable. And my sister enjoyed the celebration enough to request and display pictures, both formal and candid.

Still I didn't see my niece's marriage as the start of a new relationship, as I would Jennifer's a decade later. For my sister, what made a significant difference was the arrival of a grandson. She really enjoyed helping out, giving the parents some time off, and I daresay my niece recognized this advantage.

That doesn't particularly appeal to me, and I haven't changed my belief that Jennifer will not take well to motherhood. But it works for my sister—with the condition, she says, that some subjects are off-limits between her and her daughter. I don't even call that a condition; it's a reality I long ago accepted.

I could be wrong about Jennifer as a mother. I had no opinion about the kind my niece would make, but sitting at the table with her and her family at Jennifer's wedding brunch, I was impressed by how well her three young children behaved on their own, with little interference from a mother who had had difficult pregnancies and holds a full-time job. The kids were happy, personable, and individual, obviously a joy to her.

Although she came from the same line of mothers as Jennifer, my sister was a better mother than I, being a devoted stay-at-home mom all the time her daughter lived there. Yet my niece's role model of choice was the working stepmother she elected to live with and to help bring up a half-brother, born when she was an adolescent.

Or maybe she simply had the chance to do what an acquaintance claimed, only partly in jest, would solve mother-daughter problems. All mothers should line up opposite their daughters, who would take a step to the right to face new mothers. This would wipe out everything from bloodlines to grudges, giving both mothers and daughters a second chance.

Jennifer had that chance with her stepmother, but chance is chance, like the accident of birth to a particular mother. Her father's choice of an alternative mother didn't suit our daughter. While I chose to show and breed corgis in an effort to bring us together, my second chance at motherhood was not one I would wish on a brood bitch or me, her caregiver. I would change the accident of Poco's death, of course, but given that, I wouldn't alter the consequences by accepting a canine foster mother. At the time nursing her puppies was an imperative. No alternatives.

··*35*··

*Y*et what I did for Poco's litter was an alternative mothering experience. I have wondered if other breeders perceived raising puppies that way. Although several of the English ones I visited were married, none had children. How did they see it? I can't find out from them, and among breeders in the States whom I know better, there are few, if any, I would ask. Children being so highly prized in our culture, it might seem like an insult, a suggestion that they are compensating for some loss. Besides, many do have children as well as corgis. And there are gay and lesbian couples whose corgis may be like children to them.

In general it is a little suspect when a couple views a dog as their child. I once sold a puppy to some people who had never owned a dog but wanted a corgi. They called in the fall about getting one in the spring, when I planned to have a litter. I met them, let them see my dogs, and kept them informed through the breeding, the pregnancy, the birth. They preferred a male, and the only one turned out to be a fluffy.

I explained what kind of adult coat it would have (more like a sheltie) and offered them one of three show-quality bitches. But they took the male puppy, a bit reluctantly I thought. Then, despite my written instructions about giving him a quiet introduction to his new home, they had all their friends and relatives over to visit "this child," as they put it.

I didn't like the implications of the phrase. In order to get the gender they wanted they had to accept a "defect," yet they celebrated with a party, which frightened the puppy. When they took him to the vet, he wouldn't allow himself to be examined; the vet said he would become a fear-biter. I asked them to return him at once. Over the fence I took the puppy with one hand and gave them a check with the other.

That same day, however, I took him to my vet, where he was perfectly docile on examination; placed on the floor, he went to the vet when called, away from me. We agreed it was a bad home for a good puppy, and he eventually went to a family with two daughters and a corgi bitch, where he thrived. My vet never mentioned the "child substitute" but several breeder friends did. I wasn't sure, nor did I think it was empirically a bad thing.

I sold one of Poco's orphans to a childless couple in Virginia. They had seen Tempo, Poco's mother, vacationing with her owners. Having recently lost their red corgi, a companion to a tricolor bitch, they wanted a light red of Tempo's type. After a pleasant conversation about corgis, Tempo's "mother" told the couple I might have something available. The woman called me that same day and made a good impression.

"We're just farmers, with no children, and I'm home all day. We've had corgis for twenty years and we love them like kids," she said by way of introduction. I took to her on several counts: her devotion to the breed, her enthusiasm for my type, her modest description of their lifestyle on I don't know how many acres of gardens, not to mention forty head of black Angus. Most of all I was happy that she met a requirement I added for this particular hand-raised litter—somebody must be at home the way I had been. No working couples, *au pairs*, or dog-sitters. Every puppy would have a stay-at-home mom.

After exchanges that included a copy of my contract, photos of the puppy, and pictures of their home and grounds, we reached a happy agreement. When they came for her and took me to dinner, the wife told me they were disappointed to learn they couldn't have children, but decided that corgis and gardens would be that for them. Nothing seemed righter for this lively woman, who had just turned fifty and was obviously adored by her husband. More right, it seemed, than the current artificial alternatives.

··36··

ew people are so forthcoming as this couple about the role of corgis in their lives. When the puppy I took back was unconsciously referred to by his short-term owners as "this child," I was suspicious. Among breeders the distinctions are less clear. The one who did the tails and dewclaws on Poco's puppies, as she generously does for any within reasonable driving distance, is wholeheartedly devoted to the welfare of the breed; she will spend the night helping someone whelp a litter. But she also has two adult children.

When I met her years ago at one of my first dog shows, she struck me as the typical Westchester wife and mother. They lived in a huge house, with a puppy room over the garage. It was a spacious area for them to run around in but not ideal for socializing or training them to use the outdoors. Her office—as secretary of the national breed club—was a compact two-by-four pantry space off the kitchen. She proudly showed it to me, and indeed it was efficient, with a desk, typewriter, and bookshelves to the ceiling, all behind louvered doors that concealed it, like the puppies above the garage.

That something was wrong became apparent when her husband left her, not for a younger woman, just a different one—with no dogs. Both the children, adopted and now in their thirties, had emotional problems. Though they are financially independent and stable, my friend still caters to them and their needs.

After her divorce she bought a smaller home ideally suited to several adult corgis and puppies, who are reared to three weeks in her bedroom, then transferred to her guest room and ultimately placed on a large screened porch with easy access to a fenced puppy yard. Her adults run through acres of woods, which she herself fenced before she moved. Her extra bedroom is also set up with a computer, on which she has written books on the breed. Her priorities are apparent in this new house — except that she will take in her son when he is out of a job or keep her daughter's unruly dachshund when she and her husband go on vacation.

"They're your children," she will say, if anyone suggests she needn't be so indulgent. "You have to take care of them." That she believes and acts on this is clear, but so is the blossoming of her commitment to corgis after the divorce. I am familiar with her quandary: she still wants to be the perfect mother, an ideal I gave up when Jennifer became a legal adult at eighteen.

She recently admitted something I also understood. Like many breeders of long standing, she believed that corgis were not physically affected by hip dysplasia, as indeed they are not in the way that larger breeds are. Laxity in the hip joint does not usually cause corgis to go lame.

But a lot of us began to screen our dogs' hips in an effort to avoid potential lameness by having them X-rayed and evaluated. When our national breed club adopted this screening into its code of ethics, my friend had hers X-rayed and found that her top-producing brood bitch was dysplastic. She expressed her concern to me: "I shouldn't breed her again. I'll just have to start all over. But it's so hard, because I feel this is the one thing in my life I do well."

Although I hadn't yet raised Poco's puppies, I knew what she meant. I realized how painfully honest the statement was. Despite her tireless efforts on behalf of her family, it was obvious she felt they had failed. And though she has a B.A. from Smith and worked full-time after her divorce, it was always at clerical jobs. No wonder she runs around being the "whelper helper" and doing tails and dewclaws.

But maybe she was right not to give up on motherhood. The best bitch she ever had—and it was her own breeding—could no longer be used. She was back to square one, after twenty-five years of success with a line she had established. Even though her children weren't from her genetic line, she had something to go on with: an adult relationship with them, like the companionship of her brood bitch.

I lost Poco, but I had something I could literally go on with: Psallenda, who has good hips. I had also wanted to go on with Poco, in a fresh relationship based on our experience with her puppies, without reference to the success of her progeny. Although I didn't have that chance, I do with Jennifer. These shattering experiences for dog breeders combined to show me, as a human mother, that all was not lost with a grown daughter.

There was, in fact, a noticeable difference when Jennifer and her husband came for Mother's Day the year after Psallenda was born. She really looked at her, noticed her. "She's beautiful," she commented as she watched her move across the yard. Close up she observed what nice "pants" she had, referring to the thick white hair on the back of her hind legs. Her husband was mystified by this, as well as Jennifer's success in kneeing her down when she tried to jump up on her. "I grew up with them," she explained to him, almost as if she might be proud of the fact.

I wonder what else besides breeding dogs can give some sense of accomplishment to women with similar family problems. Our little family worked individually with psychiatrists, and all three of us with Jennifer's. This is the traditional upper-middle-class approach, which in my observation of cases I know, doesn't often result in success. What seems to work better is a kind of patience, usually on the part of a mother like my breeder friend; with the child's eventual maturation, it appears to resolve long-standing differences.

··37··

C ounseling was available to the allegedly "bad mother" who died with her children on the railroad tracks. It was the nun counselor who spoke so strongly in her defense. But a dog wouldn't have helped: another mouth to feed, another medical expense, another dependent. Though it might have made her sons happy, it would either have been another casualty on the tracks because she couldn't bring herself to separate her children from it, or she would have had to give it up and set off on a heart-breaking journey without their dog.

Twice as a child I was deprived of a dog in that way. The first time I was ten and we moved from North Carolina to Mississippi because of my father's job. My parents found a home for Brownie, our mixed breed whom Muldoon resembled. My sister and I were promised a new one after the move, but it was we who found her, a fox-terrier type we persuaded our mother to let us adopt. When we moved to Birmingham the next year, Rascal went with us, as she did the following year to Ashville. Our landlady there didn't want a dog, and I don't know what agreements were made between her and my parents.

What I do know is that when we went to my South Carolina grandmother's for Christmas, Rascal went too, but she didn't come back. They had arranged for some people to keep her until we could take her again—or that's what our parents told us. The return trip to Ashville, the third strange place I'd lived in, with Rascal as the only constant companion, was miserable. I counted the miles between me and her all the way. But I lived the rest of the year without her, until my father was permanently domiciled in South Carolina.

At first, in order for my sister and me to start school there, we lived in a rooming house, taking our meals at a boarding house up the street. While this strikes me now as an intolerable lack of privacy, the worst part at the time was that we couldn't get our dog. But the home my parents bought was available before Christmas, and the only present my sister and I wanted was Rascal. We were so persistent that my father drove us all to her caretakers, who I am sure considered her theirs. She ran around in circles of glee as we got out of the car; we put her in it and she would see me into my senior year in college, when she died at fifteen.

But Rascal's adoptive family, including several children, were clearly broken-hearted when she left. I suspect there was no communication about it until our arrival; they were country people unlikely to have a telephone. The privilege of our class, the wishes of its daughters, prevailed. Even at the time I felt bad, but not enough to understand *their* need for her. Now I do.

Although there is a distinction between a child's attachment to a pet and a fancier's commitment to a breed, we who breed on a small scale have it both ways. Our corgis are pets who also represent our adherence to the standard and cultivation of type—like works of art, as my mentor put it. Even those with large kennels usually keep new mothers and their puppies in the house. What we have in common is an inextinguishable hope that we can not only preserve but also improve on our corgis' good qualities in the next generation. It's a joke among us that as soon as a litter is born we start thinking how we will breed a bitch from it.

When Poco's puppies were out of the woods I began to think that way—but not before. And sometimes not now, though Psallenda is a beautiful specimen. This quality may mark my style of corgi as too pretty to work, but her movement is more than adequate for her needs. She even passed a herding instinct test, with sheep rather than the cows for which they're bred. Yet I feel an accountable disinclination to breed her.

I showed her for the first time at our National Specialty when she was seventeen months old—still immature enough for developmental faults and lack of training to be forgiven. Her class was at eight A.M. in the flooding aftermath of a grade 4 hurricane. Few spectators were at ringside, the dogs were judged under the tent without group or individual gaiting around the large ring, and Psallenda was one of many young bitches with muddy feet and blinking eyes. She didn't place, but a British corgi judge was watching her intently and making notes in his catalog. I had shown Pesto, her great-grandfather, under him a good ten years earlier, when he judged our regional specialty. I had undoubtedly met him, though I didn't remember the occasion or expect he would.

When we came out of the ring he told me what a beautiful bitch she was and added, "You certainly have kept your type." My indisposition to train and show her, my fear of breeding her, my gut desire to keep her as a lovely, well-bred pet—all evaporated in the sunshine of his compliment. That's why I had driven to Harrisburg on the eve of a hurricane for an outdoor specialty show, why I breed corgis, why I stick to my type, why I don't give up after a heart-breaking loss.

··*38*··

S ome people do seem to give up, but the breeder I know who did had a lot more going for her than a compliment from an English judge. She bred the top-producing male in this country; he sired fifty champions in highly selective breedings. She sold him as a puppy because she keeps only three or four corgis as house pets the way I do. Her success made her AKC prefix known all over the world; when she became a licensed judge she was immediately invited to judge many regional specialty shows and—ultimately—the National. Her loss was not a corgi but her husband, and her story represents a curious variation on the complex human-canine relationship.

Shortly after I met her almost twenty years ago, she told me they didn't have children because they chose not to. She didn't say why and I didn't ask, but I assumed she was responding to the general expectation that "normal" couples did. Or that they had decided they wanted the corgis to play that role in their lives. Though she worked full-time he had retired early, so they were able to have a litter a year with "shared parenting." She did the whelping, at which she and her bitches are very good, and took off a week to monitor the puppies; after that her husband stayed close by them until the critical three weeks passed.

The year they decided to have two litters in quick succession and then cut back for a while, her husband died, leaving her with puppies two and four weeks old. I thought they would help her through the loss: she was no longer working and could—like me and Poco's puppies later—devote herself exclusively to raising them. She had no interest, however, except to get them out of there.

With her reputation she had many people wanting show prospects, but she didn't pursue that avenue either, except to give the best bitch from the two litters to a young woman just starting out, the daughter of a corgi breeder, on a co-ownership basis. The bitch was very successful, in the ring and in the box, as we say of a fine specimen that wins and produces well. My friend has her pick of puppies from her. But so far she has declined to take one.

She still has three older adults and says she doesn't want to breed again. She admits she misses bringing puppies into the world, the part I most fear. As she explained her reasons, it wasn't the whelping she didn't want to do, though her last one involved a trip to an emergency clinic and a puppy born in the car. It was rather the raising of them, once they were out of the box and ready to be outside, the part I most enjoy. Her reasons were valid: she would have to carry however many puppies, one at a time, down two flights of outside stairs to their city back yard—and up again—without any help.

Yet I couldn't quite accept her rationale. She had taken over more difficult jobs herself, like pruning the trees. Moreover, the ground floor of their building, a large utility room with a half-bath and kitchen-size sink and counter, could easily be made habitable for her and the puppies with a futon and a pen, a few steps from the yard. How could she just forget the maternal pleasure she took in whelping, or limit her knowledge of breed type and soundness to judging corgis only at shows?

During a recent visit, when she had arranged for me to house-sit the seldom used garden apartment of her next door neighbor in San Francisco, we had leisurely conversations every evening over wine and cheese. In the course of them I was able to see the new direction of her priorities. I shouldn't have been surprised, since I had spent so much time reflecting on women and children/dogs. But I was—until I realized it was an unexpected variation on the theme. My friend was closely involved with her late husband's son and grandson, of whose existence I had no clue.

She knew about the illegitimate son before she married, she told me, but because his mother had put him up for immediate adoption, no one expected to hear from him again. He eventually traced his parents, however, and met his father the year before his death. At some point after that my friend informed his son, whom she hadn't met, and before long she knew not only him but his own family. She told me this in the context of the people I would meet at lunch the next day, but she said enough for me to realize she considered them relatives: "He's not exactly my stepson. . . . I'm not his real grandmother, so he calls me. . . ."

This surprised me more than their existence, as she had become very withdrawn in the years following her husband's death. "For all intents and purposes," she said once, "I have no family," though she does have two siblings and several nieces and nephews. I told her I felt the same, despite having a daughter. We agreed that our dogs were it, even to the point of our wanting to stay home with them on holidays. Now, over a month before Christmas, she was asking me about books suitable for a two-year-old. Oddly my one suggestion, Tasha Tudor's *Corgiville Fair*, hadn't occurred to her.

After I met them she asked me about family resemblances to her late husband. I could see some and mentioned them. Then she pulled out a photograph album that was like a picture-pedigree of four generations of males. Her father-in-law did indeed seem prepotent, right down to his great-grandson. While we discussed it like dog breeders, I was aware that there was something new—and perhaps improved for her—in our conversation.

She liked seeing a child grow and develop, she said of the stages she had observed. But it was nice just being "the grandmother" and not having full responsibility for him. She did, more than once, ask pointed questions about raising Jennifer. I answered her truthfully and always added, "You wouldn't want to do it." She agreed; but maybe I was wrong and she would have. Maybe I would or could have too, if I'd been more flexible, as I became with my stud dogs.

But who would have chosen to hand raise an orphan litter? Though I didn't, I found it immensely gratifying when I had to. What I chose to do and my friend chose not to—have a child—was, for thirty-five years anyway, not often gratifying. Yet she uncovered a thirty-five-year-old "stepson" and started a happy human family. Was this the reason she didn't want to breed corgis any more? Did she prefer to "go on" with her husband's line, not genetically but emotionally?

I was happy she had found something to live for, as she had given the impression over five years of widowhood that there wasn't much. And yet I felt betrayed somehow: were her corgis no longer her top priority? While she planned to spend Christmas with them, as we said we preferred, she had also invited her new family for the first celebration since her husband died.

··39··

I, too, was able to alter my holiday attitude. When I got home in mid-December, I asked Jennifer and her husband for Christmas dinner. They had been about to ask me, she said, and I could bring Psallenda. While it was a longer trek than I wanted to make in a day and there was no mention of our staying over, I accepted. It would be our first Christmas together since before her father died, the same year as my friend's husband. And it turned out to be the pleasantest I could remember with her.

Jennifer was at ease. Having finished her M.L.S. and found a new job as a college reference librarian, she was enjoying the two-week vacation she allowed herself before she started in January. For the first time I felt I had influenced her in a positive way by suggesting she work at the library instead of going to camp and urging her to apply to Mount Holyoke.

They spoke of buying a larger house, the market being good for selling her tiny one. What did they want, I asked. Three or four bedrooms—one for them, an office for each, and a spare. From this I calculated they didn't plan to have children, but I didn't ask. Although this very dinner represented a change in our relationship, I realized there would always be boundaries.

Other changes—in my own priorities—had become apparent in

San Francisco. Psallenda came into season four months after her last one, though the previous interval was the more normal six months. Several factors could have caused it, from the difference in light—there was one shaft of sunlight in our garden from about 11 to 12, compared to quite a bit all day, all year, in our Connecticut yard—to the presence next door of my friend's intact corgi male, who responded early to the scent of an unspayed bitch. As soon as I saw the stain, I made calculations on my calendar and compared them to notes I had taken on her previous heats. She would probably be ready to breed just before I left.

My friend and I had already talked generally about breeding her, in conversations I found easier than those about family. "I've been watching her," she volunteered. "She's too nice not to breed—that beautiful head, arched neck, length of body, level topline. They're all hard to find." I knew she was talking like a judge, and I appreciated it. I told her I wanted to go back to her mother's bloodlines after the outcross that produced her. She mentioned a dog she had judged in southern California. I suggested hers, though he was nine years old and had sired only two litters. She said later she wasn't sure I meant it but was very pleased.

Having him next door rather than across the country when Psallenda was ready to breed for a February litter seemed like a match that was meant to be, at least over chardonnay and cheese. But I would wake up at three A.M. and worry about all the problems, starting with the immediate ones, like the stud service, which is my forte in breeding corgis—when I know the dog and have my vet's help.

Would this male still be fertile, could he penetrate a maiden bitch, would he allow an artificial insemination? Would a city vet be experienced enough to read vaginal smears accurately or well-enough equipped to do the new progesterone tests that pinpoint ovulation? Should Psallenda undergo the stress of flying across the country so soon after being bred?

I wouldn't let myself worry beyond that point. But I knew worse things could happen than that the breeding didn't take. If it was too soon and his sperm weren't viable enough to catch all the eggs she dropped over the twenty-four hours of ovulation, she might conceive only one or two puppies, which might mean a C-section; they could just keep growing and not push her into labor. I was rational enough to know that statistics alone were against her suffering her mother's fate, and that breeding her young would take advantage of a uterus that had not lost its tone "from being bombarded with progesterone at every season," as a corgi breeder-vet put it in an article on whelping problems.

But if a primapara did have a section, she might reject the puppies. I didn't want to hand raise another litter, but for complex reasons: as Psallenda's only mother, I couldn't put her aside while I reared puppies that were strangers to her. I wanted her to enjoy that experience or not have it at all.

My friend understood my anxiety in a way no one uncommitted to breeding corgis ever could. She well knew the advantage to the breed of trying to get puppies from a good bitch. She also knew about loss. She agreed with my choice not to breed Psallenda then, even though her dog might not be available at her next season, let alone so close at hand. We discussed spaying her as an option for keeping her as a beautiful pet. But I couldn't face that either: it is such an absolute finality to a modest breeder with four generations of an admirable type.

She had spayed both her bitches after her husband died, though the younger one, Poco's half-sister and a similar type, was only two. I regretted that, as it is her daughter who has done so well for her young co-owner. Seeing this spayed bitch intensified my concern to keep my own intact; she was not even two. But I had foregone the opportunity to breed her at her third season and couldn't accurately predict when her next one would be.

··*40*··

I had also postponed breeding Poco, and for a combination of reasons: I couldn't decide on a stud, I wanted a spring litter, and I preferred not to miss our month in Maine. All of these factors were more complicated than they appeared, especially when I applied them to Psallenda. Because Poco was tightly bred, I could afford to take a chance and outcross her for type, without reference to bloodlines. But Psallenda and possibly her sister who died were the only puppies I would recognize as coming from their mother. So line-breeding is almost necessary for her.

Most puppy buyers want them in early summer, and I prefer that time because of the daylight available for them to be outdoors or on the porch. The weather is actually drier in the fall, and the one litter I had in late September was outside almost every day from the time they were four weeks old. But in November I was bringing them in at 4:30 as opposed to 8:30 in summer.

June, however, is my favorite month in Maine, not only because it is less expensive and I can stay longer but also because it's quieter and I get a second spring, one that includes lupine. Tempo's early March litter enabled me to go then, but it was late May when I requested the return of the puppy whose owners I had misjudged. So I was prepared to lose however much of my prepaid month I needed to find him the right home, which I was lucky enough to do a few days before the first of June.

For Poco's litter at the end of April, I gave up Maine entirely, except that on learning my little cottage was available the last week of August and only then, I took it. That single week, with just Psallenda and me, was the "perfect" one you hope for after a spring from hell, and we loved every sunny day of it. As her first trip, it was a significant bonding experience away from home. She was the same age as Poco—four months—when I first took her, Tempo, and Pesto up there. But in photographs as well as memory, Psallenda seemed happier. And so, strangely, was I.

Now a February litter from Psallenda, if all went well in the whelping, would take care of all those reasons for postponing it: the stud was linebred like Poco, the puppies would be out and about in March and evaluated and sold or retained before June. But there was another factor, besides my fear of breeding her. I liked having one corgi—her.

Back when Pesto died and I had only Poco, I began an active search for a male of similar type and bloodlines, one I could breed to her and offer at stud if he produced well. My heart was still with males, and I was tentatively planning to place her after she had a litter by a dog I hoped to keep for his lifetime, like Pesto and Paddington. I wanted a nice Poco daughter to go on with, be a companion to the new dog, and serve as a "spare."

For over a year I studied pedigrees, poring over photographs, calling breeders here and in England, in hopes of finding a puppy or adult to share my ideal home, where not only the dog but also any bitches coming to be bred to him would be treated like family. Breeders of successful young adults, including the one to whom I bred Poco, didn't want to sell them. Those with puppies sent pictures, but none of the dozens I looked at was what I wanted. Finally it became more urgent to breed Poco than buy a "helpmeet" for her (and me).

When Psallenda matured I renewed my search, but without the

same enthusiasm. Her I would never part with; she would be mine for her lifetime. This male I wanted more for her than for me: an in-house stud with whom to start a canine nuclear family. My last chance at a well-bred puppy who would grow up in time to breed her before she was three was out of the lovely bitch my friend bred and co-owned. She had offered to choose the most promising male and let me have him.

This possibility was the central focus of my trip to San Francisco, which I timed so that he would be old enough to come home with me. Yet as the day of our viewing approached, I became aware of a subtle change in my priorities. We had planned to take Psallenda so that the co-breeder could see what a pretty companion and mate the puppy would eventually have.

But it was a long drive, during which she would be in her airline crate worrying—or so I fancied—that she was getting on a plane again. Better to let her stay in it at home, where she felt comfortable in my absence. This led me to think about actually getting on the eastbound flight in a few weeks with two crates. That was not the real trouble, but rather the admission of another corgi into the team that Psallenda and I had become. I kept the last thought to myself, and my friend agreed about the wisdom of leaving her in the apartment.

The puppies were cute, as most eight-week-olds are. Of the correct-coated males with fully descended testicles there was one we both liked though he resembled somebody else in the pedigree more than his mother. When asked by the co-breeder if she wanted a puppy, my friend said she thought not, maybe next time. Such was the tacit understanding between us.

After we left she remarked that she didn't think I wanted him. I agreed, and we talked about his difference in type from what we both like. This was the first of several decisions she helped me make out there. A few days later Psallenda was in season and we had our breed-or-don't-breed-her-now discussions. Eventually we considered a big one: my moving to San Francisco.

··41··

In six weeks I came to love the city so much I might want to make it Psallenda's and my home. When I first retired I had wondered about continuing to live in the richest county of the richest state in the country, since my job no longer required it. Although I felt I was too old and indigent to buy a house or condo, I did look out of the county and even in Maine for possibilities.

I was, in fact, sorely tempted to try a winter rental in Southport, Maine, from September through June at half what I pay for my house in Southport, Connecticut. The cottage was on the water and therefore more temperate than even a few miles inland, I knew the neighbors from having stayed nearby in the summer, and there was a nice yard for Poco, who was the right age to breed. There were some decent stud possibilities within driving distance and undoubtedly some good vets to see us through the whelping. Still I chickened out.

I had never spent more than six summer weeks in that latitude and was concerned about a dark winter, when the yard arm falls around three P.M. I mentioned the idea to my vet, who was familiar with the area. "I think I would either commit suicide or become an alcoholic," he responded with his sometimes astonishing candor. He went on to tell me about some friends who moved there and nearly went crazy the first year, after which they came to love it. But I didn't hear that part.

San Francisco was different, both in seasonal and social climate, and it was a city. I loved New York during the ten years I lived there, but when I left for my job in Connecticut I was glad to get out. Our West Village neighborhood wasn't safe anymore: the police wouldn't do anything about bar brawls on our corner, treacherous crossings between the house and Jennifer's school three blocks away, or tractor trailers that parked under our windows for the night with the motors running. They did do a report when a male exposed himself to Jennifer in broad daylight, but by the time she told me and I called them, there was no chance of apprehending him.

Still there was something I liked about the city. After reading a piece in the *Times* about City Island, I drove down there with Poco, having never visited it when we lived in New York. It wasn't picture-pretty, like either of my Southports, but you could feel the presence of water everywhere, and you couldn't go far in any direction without seeing it. There were many simple little houses on small lots that would easily accommodate me and a couple of corgis. All the dogs I saw were leashed and their owners picked up after them, per New York City law. Although it was at least an hour and a half from my vet, this was a feasible trip since I didn't have to work around a teaching schedule. But with a bitch in labor and slow traffic at the bridge, there could be problems.

Closer to home (and the vet), I cruised the shoreline Connecticut towns outside Fairfield County: Milford, Branford, Guilford, Clinton. Like all affordable waterfront properties in the northeast corridor, the houses were close together, as they were on City Island. That in itself didn't bother me; it was the proximity to dogs, of which there were many in Branford, usually running loose. This I found intolerable, because even with a fenced yard my dogs would bark at or be teased by the roaming ones. And I saw a woman trying to walk a nice Brittany spaniel on a leash past a couple of aggressive-acting labs; so leash walks would also be difficult.

My six months of idle house-hunting made me aware of my priorities, which no longer include good schools, child-oriented neighborhoods, or private space inside. They do include a fenceable grassy yard, a porch or deck where the dogs can be enclosed and I can groom them, and a whelping area, which can be in a large bedroom or den, where I can also sleep and set up my computer. For over two years I have slept in the downstairs room where I raised Poco's puppies because Psallenda won't go up the steep, uncarpeted stairs. The fact that my two males had to be carried to my upstairs bedroom in their old age added another priority: a one-story house. I've often thought that all I need upstairs in the Southport house are the bathroom, closets, and chests of drawers.

I finally recognized that what I was seeking was a "last home" for me and my corgis. But I hadn't imagined I might find this in San Francisco, where—on visits to my friend over twenty years—we indulged the fantasy of picking out cute little houses that would be perfect for me and them.

··*42*··

*Y*ou hear about people who have retired wanting to stay where they are because of their doctors. In my case it's for the vet, as I told him on a postcard from San Francisco. Good doctors and satisfactory HMOs I was sure I could find there, especially since the latter change whether you like them or not.

Or you read that they want to stay near their children. This last Christmas was the first time I felt such a pull, but I also felt some resistance. Jennifer's and my relationship is at its best in one-to-one conversations about her work, the books we've read, her cats, my dogs. What has probably done most to bring us closer is e-mail; at her urging I went online and eventually warmed up to an electronic connection with her. This crosses a continent as quickly as a state line.

To hope for a lot more—like happy holidays together—is perhaps unrealistic. We never had them as a tradition, and while the two I shared with her and her husband were a great improvement over the past, I can't be sure about the future. If they were to visit me in San Francisco, there are a number of clean, moderately priced motels in our district. This would allow Jennifer and me to maintain the mutual independence we have established.

What does tempt me to remain in Southport is the neighborhood and the town. I have known most of my neighbors for many years, and we are all friendly. Being a private person, I appreciate the steady contact; otherwise I might go days without seeing or talking to anyone. Likewise my corgis have their fence friends who regularly pet or throw balls for them. And for all of us there are the people we meet when I walk them. "By their dogs ye shall know them," an elderly man walking for his health once remarked.

Others whom I know by name and sight without ever being introduced to them respect my corgis and refer people wanting a reputable breeder to me. I didn't set out to make such a name for myself in the town. My goal was simply to enjoy and produce my own type, in accord with both the breed standard and the code of ethics of our national club. It shouldn't have surprised me that the results would be noticed over the years by discriminating people who are familiar with corgis of all stripes: horse show, backyard, pet shop. But I certainly wasn't used to compliments on anything related to mothering.

I wouldn't have that luxury—a general appreciation of my breeding stock, or even of my breed—in the places where I was looking to relocate. For myself I could find intellectuals anywhere if I felt the need. But for my corgis I wanted more than people who perceived them as a tolerable indulgence.

My house-hunting was largely limited to the fall of the "sabbatical" I gave myself after I retired. I determined to breed Poco in the spring and decided to have the litter in the house that was familiar to her and set up for all phases of rearing the puppies. After her death I wanted only to sit tight with Psallenda where I was, even after her littermates had gone to their permanent homes.

But when I had the opportunity to spend six weeks in San Francisco, I was ready for a change. What emboldened me to fly Psallenda across the country was the prospect of living in a place, getting to know it with whatever corgis I had, the way I do in Maine.

Key West, to which I also fly, has never tempted me as somewhere to live year round. The dogs are my main reason: too hot for them, too isolated from corgi people, too far from the mainland, too full of flea-infested cats, both of which multiply at will and stay on the island.

··*43*··

*F*lying to San Francisco, which is dog-friendly, entailed a great deal more forethought and anxiety than the six-hour drive to Maine. But I screwed my courage, accustomed Psallenda to the airline crate at home, and limited the baggage for us both to two carry-ons and one sturdy duffel to be checked, like her.

On consultation with my vet I had tested the effects of five milligrams of Valium on her, found that it sedated her properly, and gave her one tablet before we started. I never flew with Jennifer, but in a conversation just before I left, she suggested I mention my nervousness to a flight attendant, as she herself always did. Odd that we had so seldom shared anxieties.

Following her instructions, I let it be known after I boarded that I was concerned to know my dog was on the plane. One attendant checked and said that she was, and after we took off another brought me a sticker—detached from the one on her crate—which read "Woof. I'm on board." This adventure began to resemble my phobia-conquering trip to Oxford, which marked the beginning of my commitment to breeding corgis.

After weeks of anxiety, I finally relaxed, had a glass of chardonnay with a decent dinner, and—following the sun across the continent until it went down—eventually saw the thrilling lights of San

Francisco Bay. As my friend had promised, she was at the gate, and as the airline had, Psallenda was in the nearby baggage area before we got there. The worst was over and the best was yet to be.

It was a city idyll, in a spacious three-room garden apartment in the Marina District, where all the streets are clean, all the houses are tasteful, and all the people are friendly. Even in this urban setting, our yard was quieter and cleaner than the one in Southport. And in November, there were blooming bougainvillea, fuschia, geraniums, and chrysanthemums, plus a tree laden with ripe Meyers lemons.

We could walk two blocks and see not only water but the Golden Gate Bridge, which is also in broad view when you emerge from the local Safeway or post office. Any route to them went past a well-kept park, which asked you to leash and pick up after your dog. One had "play" hours for well-behaved dogs off leash. I didn't let Psallenda do this, but we sometimes watched from the sidewalk. She could— and did—play on our terrace, tossing a ball that squeaked, one of her talking animals, or even a child's toy she found in a flower pot.

On the street she was mainly interested in people, who responded in kind, with affection and admiration, asking if they could pet her. One woman just getting home from work saw us coming down the block and waited at her door to tell me how much she liked corgis. A couple on a motorcycle, with a papillon in the basket, stopped traffic at an intersection to say how pretty she was, even as she strained at the leash to get on board herself. It seemed as if we were being welcomed like new kids in town, obviously residents, since I was walking a city-friendly dog. It was a good feeling.

I found myself happy in the relative anonymity of the neighborhood. It was a definite attraction of relocating: starting a new life in retirement where nobody knew me, asked if I was still teaching, inquired after Jennifer, noticed I looked old. A lot of people move to find less expensive housing, warmer climates, or golf. What I wanted was a fresh start.

Like me, Psallenda was happy in San Francisco. People on the street as well as my friend and my upstairs neighbors observed it. She entertained herself, attracted the kind of attention she liked, or relaxed prettily on the park bench under our camellia tree. Even the hormonal attraction between her and the male next door was expressed romantically as "love from afar," the topic of many courtly love poems.

She would watch him intently from the French door to our terrace or from the bay window next to the bed; he quietly returned her gaze through the lattice fence between our yards. This poetic attraction between Psallenda and her suitor almost erased the anxiety I felt about breeding her. But the medieval definition of courtly love begins with suffering, though joy is its goal.

Perhaps this is true of all love. I was prepared to believe it didn't include that between human beings and dogs. The latter is never the subject of love lyrics or great tragedy or grand opera. With no idealized model, we perceive our relationship with our dogs as one that prevents suffering on their or our parts. Moving Psallenda to San Francisco and being happy with her instead of staying home and having a litter might be a permanent triumph over the suffering of maternal love.

··*44*··

*O*r was there an option? Our apartment was quite big enough
for me and her: the living room was spacious and seemed
more so because of its opening onto the terrace and the garden beyond; the kitchen was well-equipped, large enough to eat in
and even work; the bedroom was also open, with a bay window over
the terrace and a long walk-in closet. Psallenda often chose this
closet as a place to sleep.

But there was not a good whelping area. Except for the kitchen
and bathroom, the apartment was carpeted, and there wasn't a corner that would accommodate a thirty-inch square plywood box,
heat lamp, milking stool, and the like. My computer would easily fit
on a two-deck table where the owner had an enormous television
set and VCR that I didn't use. And the small laundry room had
some storage space.

We also had our terrace and garden, which we could use
almost year-round in the temperate climate. The apartment thus
met all my requirements except for a place to have puppies, and it
offered a possibility I hadn't previously recognized: a city life without the baggage of my past. I considered the implicit message—
just be happy with Psallenda there. Don't breed her.

I didn't imagine the owner would want me doing this in his

apartment anyway, if indeed he would rent it to me for a year. But what if he would? And I could get the right sub-tenant for my Southport house? And Psallenda and I went on a San Francisco sabbatical? A litter at home would mean we couldn't start it for at least nine months. But twelve months out there would give me two chances to breed her before she was three.

Then what? I knew there was an answer in the back of my mind: my friend next door. Whelping is what she does best, what she misses most about breeding. She has even whelped other people's litters in her flat. She and I could whelp Psallenda there.

I have visited her when she had puppies, once arriving right after they did. Her husband met me and told me the last one of seven had just been born. By the time we got there she was washing off the bitch in a tub used exclusively for the dogs, and the puppies were waiting for both moms on white fleece in an immaculate box. All the slimy newspapers, bloody towels, and torn placentas were disposed of. When the clean, dry mother was put back in with them, they all lined up to nurse and she went to sleep. But she was wide awake to clean each one as it finished. I could see why my friend enjoyed this, looking as I was at the happy product of a good whelping.

The room was also just right, containing a sofa bed, end tables, bookshelves, the box and lamp. It was uncluttered and sunny, close to both the bathroom and kitchen. Her husband stayed in their bedroom upstairs, I slept on the living room sofa, my friend and the puppies and their mother in the den. Like her I spent a good part of the week in there watching them. San Francisco was out-side, but this was where I wanted to be.

Still the best human whelper in the world can't do a C-section. So we might have to go to the emergency clinic, as my friend had with the difficult presentation in her last litter. Emergency vets are often more skilled at that, since it is par for their course. Or we could make arrangements in advance with a suburban vet used by any one of several long-time breeders in the Bay area. Despite the postcard I'd sent my vet in Connecticut, to the effect that I would move to San Francisco in a minute except for him, I realized he could give me names out there, as he had in Maine, or consult with me by phone for advice on a course of action.

After my friend and I whelped the puppies in her room, if she agreed, I would sleep there with them—on Psallenda's account as well as theirs—for the first three weeks. My friend would stay upstairs, where she has a fenced area on the roof that her dogs could use while the den was a maternity ward. Assuming she was amenable, then what?

A summer litter could be outside almost all the time after about five weeks because it never rains then. In fact, the overhang from the bay window in my room might even be suitable for a puppy enclosure during the night: I could hear and see them from my bed, as if they were inside. Or I could house them overnight with a gate in the very large stall shower. As they grew on, they could have full use of the terrace after I puppy-proofed it. Immediate neighbors who admired both Psallenda and my friend's corgis would help socialize them. With both of our contacts, there would be no problem selling the pets—after we selected the best for ourselves.

If all this were feasible and actually done, the experience might jumpstart my friend's breeding instinct. There might be a nice puppy for each of us, and Psallenda would, I think, enjoy her son or daughter. In that retirement scenario a brood bitch would revive the maternal joy of two breeders whose devotion to corgis included suffering that human beings and dogs do not associate with love.

• ● ● •

··45··

*T*hat breeding didn't happen, any more than Psallenda's romance with the dog next door ended in a happy marriage and family. The owner of our apartment retired from his traveling job and moved into it. San Francisco would have to become a treasured memory, like Psallenda's courtly lover.

Reality aside, there was another reason the breeding I imagined wouldn't do. If I bred her I wanted those magic first three weeks—which I lost with Jennifer and gained with Poco's puppies—all to myself and not in my friend's flat. Psallenda should nurture her litter in the familiar dog room of our Southport house, where she herself was raised.

I grew increasingly fond of this room as I painstakingly put the book about her, her mother, my daughter, and me onto the computer, learning to use it as I went along. More dispassionately I marveled at the convenience of modern technology: having typed my legal pads into a draft of single-spaced lines, with double spaces between paragraphs, I transformed that into a double-spaced manuscript with indented paragraphs by giving those instructions and "Select All."

Composing itself remained as heart-wrenching as deciding to breed, but the mechanics so improved the process that it was a natural step to consider a chilled semen procedure for Psallenda, in order to use a stud in Michigan, where I wouldn't ship her. The dog's bloodlines and type complemented hers, and he was producing well. Keeping everything mechanical, I e-mailed his owner of my interest.

One thing led to another, she came into season in October, and when a series of progesterone tests indicated she was ready to ovulate, the stud's vet collected and FedEx'd his semen to one in Connecticut who specializes in such inseminations. The sample looked good, she said, then impregnated Psallenda with a syringe and pipette. This was by no means a romantic encounter, nor did it even seem real—until I was driving home and thought, What have I done?

Up to then I had figured that if I got scared, despite the agony of deciding to breed and all the money I'd spent on blood tests, vaginal smears, collection kits, FedEx, and the stud fee, I could— at the last minute—say "Don't do it." Not now. Still I was more excited than afraid, until I learned my vet would be away the week she was due to whelp. What if she needed a C-section? Mine was among the few who respected the high mortality rate of corgi bitches and puppies and the only one who would get up in the middle of the night to do one for me.

With the information I had from vaginal smears and progesterone tests, I could be fairly certain about the gestation period, which is traditionally nine weeks from the first mating. But that could be several days before ovulation or two or three after. With shipped semen you aim for a couple of days afterward, in order to fertilize the eggs just when they mature; whelping is sixty-three days after ovulation. That might put Psallenda's due date at January 6, the day my vet was leaving. Alternatively, if you know from vaginal cytology the day she went completely out of estrus, you can count eight weeks from that, which would make it January 5, his last day. A large litter might come earlier, and all dates are give or take twenty-four hours.

Although it is unwise to do an elective C-section on a maiden bitch except for medical reasons—which Psallenda's narrow pelvis might constitute—I was hoping she would be close enough to term before my vet left for him to save her and the puppies that way. I couldn't count on Mother Nature, who in my experience is not a good one, especially if she deserts you when your surgeon is gone.

Psallenda didn't look very big when we X-rayed her six weeks into pregnancy; indeed, we could see only two spines. Definitely not a big litter. I was disappointed at first. They wouldn't come early, she might need a section, and two didn't give me a lot to choose from. But as I watched Psallenda being her usual happy self, never missing a meal or looking uncomfortable, I was grateful for her small load. The only sign she gave of her condition was to pamper herself by taking her ease on my bed—my pillow even—when I wasn't in it. Maybe bitches do know when they're pregnant and are pleased about it, the way I was.

During the last week I monitored her temperature, which runs about a degree lower than the average 101, then drops to 99 or below and doesn't go up in the course of the day. On January 4, when I'd scheduled an ultrasound to determine the size and viability of the pups, it was just over 99 in the morning, the lowest yet, but I never checked it again. The puppies were big, with good heartbeats, and she had milk as well as a relaxed vulva, though she'd shown none of the textbook signs of imminent labor—no digging about in the box, no panting, no vomiting.

We decided to keep the tentative appointment for a section the next day. A snowstorm was on the way, so rather than drive home and back again, I spent the night with the friends who adopted Tempo and lived nearby. What surprised me was my decision to leave Psallenda at the hospital in case she did go into labor. But veterinary technology was what had got me this far in breeding her, and now I felt I had to rely on it exclusively. I *did* say good-bye as she trotted off happily with an attendant; I even added, "Now don't die."

But I hardly slept and was alarmed when the vet called and said, "Once again a surprise," though I should have known he wouldn't preface bad news that way. It was a good surprise. After she was shaved and prepped for surgery and he turned her over to inject her, she had a puppy. An hour later she had the other, both healthy, a dog and a bitch. So that was the trick, I decided driving back to the hospital: leave her to her own devices, without me, Mother Nature, oxytocin, or surgery, and she'd do it her way, perhaps achieving what all mothers want.

Before she was discharged I got into the ground-level compartment with Psallenda and made sure the puppies could nurse. She had been allowed to lick them, but—at my request—they hadn't been put in alone with her as I didn't quite trust a primapara's instincts. The male caught on right away, and the female did after I let her suck good and hard on my little finger. We packed up and set off, Psallenda whining in her crate and them squealing in the cooler on a water-filled glove they knew wasn't their mother.

··46··

When we got home I was in for another surprise. I took the puppies in first, transferred them to the big whelping box, and turned on the heat lamp. Then I let Psallenda relieve herself in the yard and wiped her all over with a warm wet towel, after which I allowed her to go to the nest. She looked at it, walked to her toy basket, collected her six farm animals (not my violin), put them in her own crate, and joined them. Some maternal instinct.

I didn't try to take the toys away, but if I had to leave the room, I closed the crate, which she didn't appear to mind. Later, when I was ready to settle in with the puppies, I put them in the cardboard changing box and lured her to the big plywood one, where she'd been sleeping for two weeks. Holding her head I put one puppy on her. At first she whined, but shortly she relaxed and went to sleep. I did the same with the other, then both. I didn't leave my milking stool beside her, but I did take my hand off her head.

She had been licking their bellies, mostly the tied umbilical cords, but when I saw one puppy defecate I presented its rear to her. She reacted as I might: I'm supposed to *eat* that? So I did it my way, with a baby wipe. She was taking care of the urine, I noticed.

When I contemplated going to bed I realized I would be up

every couple of hours as I had been with Poco's litter, the difference being that I didn't have to make the food. *And I still had Psallenda.* But I didn't think she was ready to be left unattended with her puppies. So they stayed in their separate boxes except when I got up to supervise feedings. I didn't sleep; they were noisier than *my* puppies, perhaps because they knew what they were missing.

With each feeding Psallenda seemed to get better at the whole job: she licked her puppies all over, then sat up so they could crawl under her to nurse. Eventually I saw her stimulate and clean up their stools. With so much progress on her part and so little sleep on mine, I finally let her stay with them in the early hours of her first day as a full-time mother. All was quiet and everybody slept.

But after I fed her, let her out, and changed the bedding, she surprised me again. When I handed her a puppy she growled, for the first time in her life. I scolded her and carefully put both puppies on her, holding her head. After they nursed I watched closely as she cleaned them. When I reached to pick one up, she snapped at me, then bared her teeth. So that was it: she was protecting her brood. Though I accepted her attitude, I shook her by the scruff of the neck and said *"No."* After that she allowed me to share them, but I didn't forget my secondary place in the rearing of these, Psallenda's, babies.

In her brood bitch role she didn't go back to the crate with her animals, but I was startled the next day to see something non-corgi in the whelping box—the rooster. I surreptitiously removed it, and in the same manner she put it back. At that point I decided it wasn't doing any harm, being clean and nontoxic, so I left it. I eventually saw a puppy nuzzled next to it.

The natural mother had still more in mind. Later she brought in the goat and placed it and the rooster with the puppies in front of her. My only concern about her beloved animals, on which she liked to suck and knead—presumably because she hadn't been able to on her mother—had been that she would do the same on her puppies' limbs. But she knew better than that; with the corgi's celebrated mind of her own, she was integrating her family.

Eventually—when Psallenda was less inclined to be with her babies all day and night—I was successful in keeping the farm animals out of the box. The puppies needed more space because they were big, perhaps too big, from "overmothering," an indulgence I can only admire. Human intervention is sometimes necessary, however, to prevent them from becoming fat and flat and not walking when they should. *My* puppies were walking at two weeks, before their eyes opened, and they could see where they were going. If hers weren't by three weeks, I was prepared to "hobble" their rear legs with tape and a single strip of rubber band between them so that they are forced to use them. But I decided not to mind Psallenda's business. After it dawned on me that I was feeding her too much for two puppies, they got up and were walking before they were three weeks old.

They also moved from the box to the pen before that time because in the middle of one night I heard a lot of fussing and wondered why Psallenda didn't do something about it—let the puppy out of a corner or sit up to give it easy access to a teat. Finally I turned on the light and saw one of them walking across the floor. To contain them I put up the open side of the box and left her out. Every mother knows that too close confinement with no escape is bad, but Psallenda hadn't learned that and I didn't want her to under my watch.

I spent several hours the next morning setting up the indoor pen, this time with a covered foam pad at one end for Psallenda and newsprint at the other, which the puppies knew to urinate on after one experience in the box, when the volume was apparently too much for their mother. That done, I put them in it while I took the whelping box out of the room. They were not one bit happy, but I had to finish the job before allowing Psallenda back in: she would be upset to see her nest taken away.

When I finished I saw I was mistaken. She went right to the pad, they followed, climbed on it, and happily nursed. She didn't even get excited when I vacuumed the room. She knew her role, and my shoving furniture around wouldn't have bothered her.

··47··

I had never observed a brood bitch closely enough to appreciate her superior mothering, except in retrospect, when I did her job myself, so much better than I had done my own with Jennifer. Amazing, then, that Psallenda—nurtured by me—was a brood who knew exactly what she was doing, even with her eccentricities. Especially with them.

Not only had I become a good mother with Poco's puppies but I had also produced one, against all odds. Psallenda never knew her own mother, she free-whelped two big puppies on an operating table, she transferred her affection for her farm animals to her babies overnight, she gave them priority over me but accepted my partnership in rearing them. I in turn understood her as a mother, a single mother.

I pondered the ideal of a nuclear family bred from love: that had perhaps been my undoing, at least my belief that after having a baby my husband and I would live happily ever after. Though I wouldn't do it myself, I can understand women who have or adopt a child on their own, without any family trappings, to enjoy motherhood and child-rearing. Psallenda's FedEx stud may be best way for a bitch to do the same thing. She had had her romantic adventure in San Francisco. Back in a cold Connecticut winter she was content with her brood in the house where she was raised.

I can also see why many mothers want to breed a litter in order for their children to see "the miracle of birth." I strongly disapprove of breeding for that reason, and I told a neighbor who spoke of doing it with a pet corgi that she wouldn't want them to see her die like Poco. I deliberately said this in front of her youngest daughter; they both heard me and the bitch was spayed. I myself missed the birth miracle with Psallenda, but I did, in the three weeks with which I am so familiar, observe a miraculous motherhood.

I was, in fact, more fascinated with her than the puppies during that time. But I began watching them more attentively after they were half-weaned at five weeks, when Psallenda still nursed them at bed-time. Both puppies were attractively marked, had correct coats, and pretty heads. The male was chunky while the female had her mother's longer outline and neck. He was definitely more laid-back; I noticed it as soon as I weighed them—he was still, she squirmed. She was smarter, too, as many bitches are, being the first to bark, just once, as if to show she could do it. She sometimes got fresh with her mother, scrapping with her like a sibling, whereas the male was submissive to her.

I watched closely to see how Psallenda disciplined them: she placed a paw on the puppy's back, then nosed it with her head. The male lay down and turned over, supine and submissive. The female sat down, and after more nosing, lay down, but on her side, curled up, ready to spring, it appeared. Once she did spring, snarling at her mother, as opposed to squabbling with her brother. Psallenda nosed her again, with more patience than I thought was warranted. The puppy only sat down; her mother came to the edge of the pen and I let her out.

Despite my wish to buy or breed a nice male, Psallenda changed my preference for that gender in corgis. It isn't just her dependence and affection, qualities I've found more abundant in dogs than in bitches; it is what she has taught me, beyond what I was obliged to learn from her mother's death. Not only her mothering, but her extending the maternal bond both ways: from me to the puppies, from them to me. She used to sleep lightly on my bed, jumping down if I turned over, then coming back up until I moved again. Now she settles like a rock, not budging when I try to change my position. I interpret this as a need for and desire to give reassurance.

We seemed to want to reassure each other about keeping her daughter. "Psalm could be a problem," I said aloud to Psallenda on the bed. She had refused to even lie down after a gentle rebuke for impertinence, and her mother had come to me in frustration. "She's not a bad puppy," I went on. "It's natural to get mad at your mother. But she's not like you, and we might all be happier if she lives somewhere else. We can keep Potus instead, even if he isn't a show dog." We both slept on my maternal words. I was determined to be a good mother to her for the rest of her life.

For all my dubious human mothering, my daughter is now happy, not only with her husband and job, but in the big old house they bought and are renovating. Psallenda's grandmother, Tempo, who didn't like her daughter Poco, is also happy in her adoptive home, unaware that she is dying of cancer. Her owners didn't have the chance to get Poco, but they will soon have Psalm to keep them "young and laughing."

And to keep Psalm and Psallenda from fighting. Bitch fights, of which I have never seen any among corgis, are said to be worse than those between dogs, presumably because they have no reason—like male dominance—to fight. Whatever the reason females do it, I know enough about mothers and daughters to protect Psallenda from an adult relationship in which there is no hope for the reconciliation I have finally achieved with my daughter.

The human-canine bond is justly praised for differences in favor of the dog, but my experience with bitches tells me it is a subtle similarity between a brood bitch and a human mother which is the ultimate tie that binds. Not the physical tie in a natural mating, not the legal one of marriage, not the umbilical cord tying mother and daughter. Not those at all, but a shared sense of the awesome obligations, frustrations, and rewards of motherhood.